à Lisa Roma, cantatrice, musicienne et artiste
Maurice Ravel Février 1928

THE SCIENCE
and
ART OF SINGING

by

LISA ROMA, M. Mus.

Professor of Singing
University of Southern California (1930-1931-1932)

1956 — Adjunct Professor of Voice
University of Southern California

G. SCHIRMER, Inc.
New York

DEDICATION

To my dear husband, for his encouragement
while writing this book.

CONTENTS

ILLUSTRATION

Frontispiece: Maurice Ravel and Lisa Roma

DIAGRAMS

v

Lisa Roma, an American soprano born in Philadelphia, has gained international recognition. She started out as a protege of David Bispham, studied with Trabadello in Paris and Max von Schillings in Berlin. Maurice Ravel chose her to interpret his songs on his American tour.

She has sung leading roles in the Staats-Opera of Berlin and the Philadelphia Grand Opera Company and has appeared with the Boston, Philadelphia, Chicago, Cleveland and San Francisco Symphony Orchestras — besides having sung with such famous artists as Gigli, Tibbett, Schumann-Heink, John Charles Thomas, Casals and many others. She holds the degree of Master of Music and was Professor of Singing at the University of Southern California.

Lisa Roma sang at the opening of the first radio station in Philadelphia and also sang at the first multiple tie-up in the United States of six radio stations from WJZ New York. She is still singing and recording arias, songs and lieder.

FOREWORD

This is a manual for singers!

This is not a treatise to be read casually from cover to cover at one sitting. It is a manual condensed to its irreducible minimum form, a system of Voice Production based on purely scientific principles. It is so basic and fundamental that it will never need revision.

The purpose of this book is to stress chiefly the scientific voice production in the art of singing. Diagrams and explanations of the vocal organs and adjacent parts, as well as acoustics and other related matters have been explained and described in many books dealing with the subject matter.

Therefore, I have tried to keep this treatise concise and explicit, and to eliminate all extraneous matter, and by its purposeful brevity to avoid confusing the student with irrelevant subjects.

This manual should be studied chapter by chapter in order to properly absorb and apply the instructions contained therein. It should be used as a reference book throughout your entire singing career.

The subject of the science of correct breathing as related to singing has been treated repetitiously — and deliberately so — in my effort to impress upon the reader, whether he be a student, teacher or artist, that scientific breathing is 95 per cent of singing.

By eliminating all complex and professional terminology, I have deliberately simplified all explanations in my effort to impart the physical and esthetic sensations involved in singing.

THE SCIENCE AND ART
OF SINGING

CHAPTER I

The object of science is knowledge. The object of art is works.

Science is the knowledge of facts, coordinated, arranged and systematized.

Art begins where science leaves off and when the science is completely understood and absorbed.

The science of voice production is a knowledge of certain phenomena of physical movements, which are found under certain conditions to occur regularly and which produce certain definite effects.

We should never lose sight of the fact that there is a true science of voice production and that the art of song is based upon this science. There is only one way to sing perfectly and that is the correct scientific way.

It is my desire to help other serious singing artists, or potential artists, to reach a goal for which all singers strive; to sing beautifully and well, and to preserve the singing voice.

The preservation of the singing voice is necessary and possible, and you should be able to sing as long as you are able to breathe.

1

Withholding my knowledge of singing cannot enrich me. I am amply rewarded and gratified to impart what I know if by so doing we can develop a nation of fine singers, as I am convinced we already have the finest natural voices in the world.

So far as the scientific production of the voice is understood in its entirety, *it can be proved*, and will show forth the reward of a perfect singing voice.

This process entails hard and dedicated thinking, and harder and more dedicated work.

I shall analyze scientifically the causes and effects of the production of sound in the human voice.

To begin with, all singing must of necessity be beautiful, first, last and always. Rather have it said that the voice is small and beautiful than loud and otherwise.

The small beautifully placed voice is capable of portraying the full gamut of human emotions.

Therefore, it is necessary to develop *our own instrument*, which is the vocal apparatus we rely upon to produce our own beautiful singing.

When singing is most scientifically produced, and the voice soars out smoothly, evenly and vibrantly, with its resultant seeming effortless singing, that is when critics will pronounce you a *naturally* perfect singer, with a natural legato.

The greatest art in singing is *simplicity* and concealing the artifice required to achieve this *ostensible simplicity*.

In order to form a basis for the meeting of our minds, and to have a mutual understanding, we must first formulate exact definitions of all terms relating to our subject matter. When you read my words, you will know exactly what I am referring to and how I use them because the same words have different connotations for each person.

Figure 1

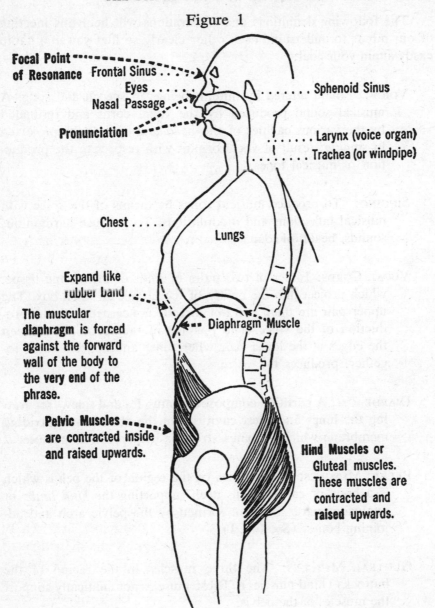

Focal Point
of Resonance ····· Frontal Sinus ···

Eyes ·······

Nasal Passage

······· Sphenoid Sinus

Pronunciation ····

····· Larynx (voice organ)

····· Trachea (or windpipe)

Chest ·····

Lungs

Expand like
rubber band ····

The muscular
diaphragm is forced
against the forward
wall of the body to
the very end of the
phrase.

····· Diaphragm Muscle

Pelvic Muscles ······
are contracted inside
and raised upwards.

Hind Muscles or
Gluteal muscles.
These muscles are
contracted and
raised upwards.

The following definitions and illustrations will help this meeting of our minds to understand each other clearly so that you may more easily attain your goal:

VOICE: Sound uttered by human beings in speech and song. A musical sound produced by the vocal cords and resonated by the various cavities of the head and eyes. Tone projected in singing; result of vocal organs with respect to the production of musical tones.

SINGING: To produce musical tones by means of the voice with musical inflections and modulations. To produce harmonious sounds, beautiful sounds.

VOCAL CORDS: Either of two pairs of folds of membrane tissue, which project into the cavity of the larynx or voice box. The upper pair are thick and not directly concerned with the production of the voice. The passage of breath or air between the edges of the lower pair when tense and approximated together, produces the voice.

DIAPHRAGM: A partition composed of muscles and sinews separating the lungs and chest cavity from the abdomen; a dividing membrane which becomes stronger with practice and use.

PELVIC MUSCLES: The muscles of the region of the pelvis which is a bony or cartilaginous arch supporting the *hind limbs* or analogous parts. In man, formed by the pelvic arch and adjoining bones. (See Fig. I)

GLUTEAL MUSCLES: The three muscles in the region of the buttocks (hind muscles). These muscles automatically support the muscles of the pelvis.

Figure 2

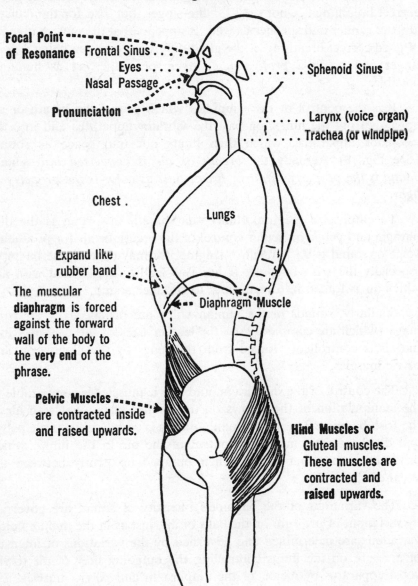

Focal Point
of Resonance Frontal Sinus
                Eyes
            Nasal Passage

Pronunciation

Sphenoid Sinus

Larynx (voice organ)
Trachea (or windpipe)

Chest .

Lungs

Expand like
rubber band

The muscular
diaphragm is forced
against the forward
wall of the body to
the very end of the
phrase.

Diaphragm Muscle

Pelvic Muscles
are contracted inside
and raised upwards.

Hind Muscles or
Gluteal muscles.
These muscles are
contracted and
raised upwards.

Control of the diaphragm and pelvic muscles is the secret of good, correct breathing . . . not only for the singer, but also for the dancer, athlete, runner and speaker as well. It appears that the elusive obvious of good correct breathing, is the great difference between being a *good* singer and being a *professional* singer, or as perfect as humanly possible.

It is the control of these muscles which propel the breath or air upwards from the lungs, on past the vibrator apparatus and into the resonator apparatus, which then floats out into space as sound. (See Fig. 1) Actually the *breath or air is converted into sound. Sound is the property of air or breath just as color is the property of light.*

To emphasize the importance that breathing — that is the diaphragm and pelvic muscular control of the breath or air for producing voice or sound is 95 percent of singing, we may observe the bagpipe, especially the Irish bagpipe. It has two leather bags, filled with air, which air is forced into reed pipes to produce sound.

Similarly, sounds of the human voice are produced by air from lungs (which are comparable to the leather bags of the bagpipe) and the air is controlledly forced from the lungs by the diaphragm and pelvic muscles.

The control of the diaphragm and pelvic muscles is comparable to the manipulation of the elbows on the leather bags filled with air in the Irish bagpipe. This elbow manipulation is comparable to the pelvic and diaphragmatic muscular control of the air in the lungs, which produces sound (our voice) when pumped up gently between the vocal cords.

The variations of the bagpipe's intensity of sound are governed by variations of pressure on the bags of air, just as in the human voice, variations are determined and governed by the variations of intensity of pressure on the lungs controlling the outgoing flow of air to the vocal apparatus by means of the diaphragm and pelvic muscles.

Like the lungs, the leather bags have a fixed diameter and circumference, which must be expanded to their full capacity. When expanded, the air rushes into the bagpipe and when pressed on by the elbows, the air is compressed and expelled into the reeds at a rate and intensity directly proportionate to the pressure applied to the bags.

Likewise, the lungs, also, have a fixed diameter and circumference. You merely expand them to their maximum capacity or diameter, and the air rushes in by its own weight and pressure of 14.7 pounds per square inch. Then the air is expelled by the pressure applied by the diaphragm and controlled by the pelvic and gluteal muscles.

The quality, intensity and emotional interpretation of sound (your voice) is totally dependent upon the muscular control and the pressure applied to the lungs (human bellows) which provides air that produces sound (voice), reflecting the true art of muscular control. The result of this process is the *major portion* of the true science of voice production.

Let me reiterate: *breathing,* is the most important factor for the singer to *study and consider*. Really, the first step in singing and the most important one is a thorough knowledge of breathing. I consider breathing to be about 95 percent of the science of singing. The other 5 percent is the *proper placement of the air* which is converted into sound or our voice.

Figure 3

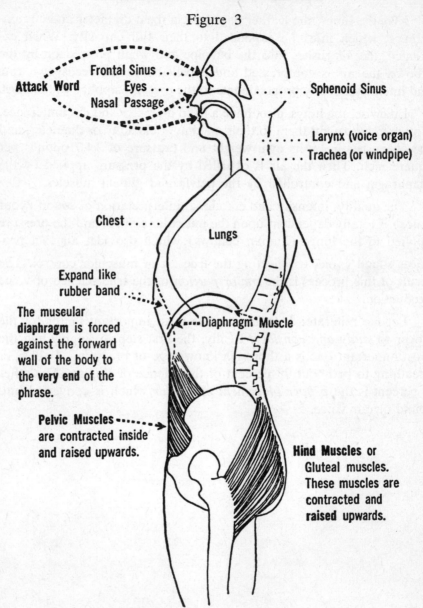

Frontal Sinus . . . . .

Attack Word   Eyes . . . . .

Nasal Passage . . . . .

. . . . Sphenoid Sinus

. . . . Larynx (voice organ)

. . . . Trachea (or windpipe)

Chest . . . . .

Lungs

Expand like
rubber band . . . . .

The museular
diaphragm is forced
against the forward
wall of the body to
the **very end** of the
phrase.

. . . . Diaphragm Muscle

Pelvic Muscles . . . .
are contracted inside
and raised upwards.

Hind Muscles or
Gluteal muscles.
These muscles are
contracted and
raised upwards.

CHAPTER II

BREATHING FOR VOICE PRODUCTION

The basic formula for correct breathing is a co-ordinated combination and control of muscles and tissues, and a natural and easy attitude of the body so that the breath or air has free passage through the vocal apparatus to be transformed into beautiful sound.

The easy and persuasive attitude of the body while singing, is acquired by having the body perfectly poised: arms loosely dangling and relaxed, lower jaw loosely dropped away from the face.

Avoid rigidity and discomfort of any kind.

Balance on the balls of the feet and heels.

Avoid all mannerisms, habits and idiosyncrasies.

There are six steps in the act of correct breathing to consider:

1. SPINE STRAIGHT
2. SHOULDERS DRAWN BACK AND DOWN
3. CHEST HIGH AND IMMOVABLE
4. STOMACH DRAWN IN
5. DIAPHRAGM EXPANDED LIKE A STRETCHED RUBBER BAND
6. PELVIC MUSCLES RAISED AND SUPPORTED BY GLUTEAL MUSCLES (See Fig. 3)

After Steps 1, 2, 3 and 4 are complied with, we are ready for Step 5. The diaphragm muscle should be expanded to the utmost, like a taut, elastic band; creating a vacuum in the lung and chest cavity, allowing the air to automatically fill the lungs due to the atmospheric pressure of 14.7 pounds per square inch. You will be aware of this physically, by the expansion in the area of the waistline.

Air is not drawn or sucked in. You simply make room for the air to *flow* in, as in opening a door to a room, the air is not drawn in, it fills all space in the room automatically.

The muscular diaphragm is forced against the forward wall of the body to the *very end* of each phrase.

Step 6: Simultaneous with the expansion of the diaphragm muscle is the contraction and raising of the muscles of the pelvic region, *lifting* and *holding firm* the pelvic muscles continuously while singing.

Going back to our definition of the *pelvic muscles,* you will note in the diagram (page 8) the underscoring of the words *hind muscles.* These *gluteal* or *hind muscles* in turn support the muscles of the pelvis. These must be held firm and not allowed to relax at any time while the tones are being produced.

The singer who follows these directions, will be immediately surprised at the additional breath he or she has in reserve.

After these muscles are held firmly then curve the small of the back forward and inward, press the diaphragm firmly against the floating ribs and forward wall. The diaphragm does not collapse until after the singing ceases.

This basic combination is what we call correct breathing.

This same formula of breathing applies to all voices, from the coloratura soprano to the deepest bass voice.

Operatic stars are able by this diaphragm and pelvic breathing to project tones that carry to the largest audience, over a full dominant orchestra, even though they may be kneeling or reclining on the stage.

After the breathing apparatus is perfected so that it obeys your will, you may next consider singing.

The most valuable help to the singer, however, is first to study this simple and natural method of breathing. Study it physically, and mentally, until it becomes a natural part of you.

Singing is the *controlled flow of breath* through the vocal cords, hitting the resonating chambers of the eyes, nose and sinuses like hammers hitting on bells or mallets on a xzylophone, (as air and breath striking the walls of brass or wood instruments.) This controlled flow of breath vibrates and flows upward, to form sound, while supported by the aforementioned breathing process.

Breath becomes voice by the steady flow of air through the vocal cords and voice box, *and* the co-ordination of the vocal organs and resonating chambers.

The latter are actually the sound-board of the human voice.

This entire *co-ordinated physical process of breathing and the transformation of the breathing into sound, is the instrument of the singer.*

This instrument of the singer does not include the heart and soul needed for the interpretation of music. This physical instrument or process of breathing and placing the voice should become so automatic that it will be second nature to the singer. It must obey the will of the artist, just as an instrumentalist must first have a perfect instrument on which to perfect his technique before he can truly interpret his music.

BREATHING EXERCISES FOR MUSCULAR CONTROL

DIAPHRAGM EXERCISES:

1: Expand diaphragm.

2: Raise pelvic and gluteal muscles and let the air rush in like a deluge. The lungs are now filled like a blown up balloon.

3: The chest and shoulders must not move even a particle.

Let the outside natural forces of air pressure send the air in. You do not have to draw or suck the air in. Your part is simply to make room for the air to flow in. The sensation is that of being gently blown up like a balloon. Then draw in the diaphragm sharply, quickly and hard, until it seems to touch the spine. Expand again until the diaphragm is forced against the forward wall of the body, draw in again over and over. Repeat this exercise while standing, sitting, walking or reclining.

This exercise will strengthen the diaphragm muscle to such a degree that it will always obey your will.

PELVIC MUSCLE EXERCISE

Regular scheduled brisk walking is the best exercise for strengthening the pelvic muscles, simultaneously exercising the diaphragm as described above.

This diaphragm and pelvic controlled breathing process is what forms the natural *legato* of singing; holding the voice in a firm, straight melodic line without any extra effort having to be applied, thereby taking all pressure away from the throat, which remains relaxed and open.

The natural legato is accomplished only when the pelvic and diaphragm muscles are responsive to your commands. This will only be attained after a period of many months when diligent exercise (including calisthenics) has rendered them strong and flexible.

When these muscles are strong and flexible they will obey your every command quickly and delicately and they are easily controlled. You can then measure out and minutely control the *necessary breath in an even flow which creates the natural legato.*

This natural legato allows the voice to pour out evenly on and with the breath, like a string of matched pearls, or a string of Christmas tree lights, brilliant and vibrant.

The "metering out" effect of the breath in an even flow can be increased and decreased by manipulation of the pelvic muscles for varying tones, to create dramatic effects as well as crescendos and decrescendos to color and vitalize the voice.

Merely by developing and maintaining the diaphragm and pelvic muscles in strong condition as the result of much exercise you can build them up to the required strength. This is, of necessity a time-consuming and tediously slow process.

It cannot be rushed! No muscle, whether it be an arm or leg muscle or the pelvic muscle, can become strong and flexible except by a slow building-up method.

I cannot caution you enough to use every effort and good judgement in this muscular control building, that it be done gradually over an extended period of time in order not to strain the muscles. (Make haste slowly.)

You must realize that you are building a foundation for thirty or forty years of singing. A few years spent on careful preparation to build this foundation should not be considered a sacrifice of *time* or *effort*. It can pay tremendous dividends!

You must be as exacting as an athlete. Make sure, after due test, that your diaphragm and pelvic muscles, especially for female singers, are in condition. They must be flexible and strong to endure the task you assign them. At all times they must be under your complete control no matter how taxing the particular vocal work you propose to perform.

Do not attempt, in your training stage, (or for that matter throughout your professional career), to sing a performance that will require more muscular strength and physical stamina than you are prepared for at that time.

This careful muscular control will take all strain away from the throat and vocal cords.

Regardless of whether the tone sung is a high or a low note; whether the tone is sung fortissimo, piano or pianissimo; whether the tone is sung briefly or elongated; whether staccato or legato; in rapid cadenzas or long, sustained tones, the voice should always retain the resounding ring or vibrancy of all the resonating cavities of the eyes, sinuses and nasal passages.

LEGATO: A continuous melodic line, a joined melody.

STACCATO: A detached tone-separated melodic line.

Care should be taken not to call anything by name, such as "inhale" or "exhale", unless we bear in mind the scientific function of the diaphragm and pelvic muscles, lest we be tempted to "draw in" or "blow out" air. "Inhale" and "exhale" mean different functions to different people. It is best not to use these terms until the scientific meaning of "inhale" and "exhale" are thoroughly and completely understood.

INHALE: Expand the diaphragm muscle like a rubber band and press out against the forward wall of the body.

EXHALE: Collapse the diaphragm and pull the muscle in, until it seems to touch the spine. (See Fig. 4)

Figure 4

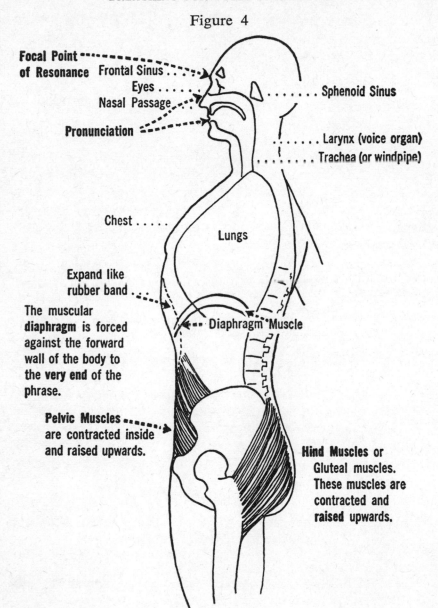

Focal Point
of Resonance   Frontal Sinus
                    Eyes
                Nasal Passage

Pronunciation

Sphenoid Sinus

Larynx (voice organ)
Trachea (or windpipe)

Chest

Lungs

Expand like
rubber band

The muscular
diaphragm is forced
against the forward
wall of the body to
the **very end** of the
phrase.

Diaphragm Muscle

Pelvic Muscles
are contracted inside
and raised upwards.

Hind Muscles or
Gluteal muscles.
These muscles are
contracted and
raised upwards.

CHAPTER III

THE APPLICATION OF
BREATHING IN SINGING

The voice is not a series of disembodied sounds, it is our instrument which we must perfect and play upon in order to produce beautiful song.

Singing is not only the science of voice production, but also requires the expression of the body, voice, mind and heart, to interpret the composer's and poet's inspiration and expression of music and text.

We sing not only with the voice, but also with our entire body, soul, mind and being.

This incorporation of the body, soul and mind with the voice, is the impelled and/or propelled air sent up and out, by the breathing apparatus.

This apparatus must be trained to obey our will. The body must serve the singer's purpose freely and without hindrances.

17

During the process of breathing, (which I have explained in great detail in the previous chapter), the entire body should be relaxed, the arms dangling, the throat and neck muscles relaxed. The chest should never be allowed to collapse or drop, but should remain high, even during *acting; whether walking, standing, sitting, reclining, bending* or *dancing.*

This process of breathing is entirely different from the accepted method of breathing. *It is purely muscular.*

Do not consciously breathe through the nose or mouth but *utilize both* naturally and you should get the required air or breath by distending and expanding the diaphragm muscle and raising the pelvic and gluteal muscles.

Place your hand on your diaphragm when you breathe. You will then feel the expansion in the entire area of the waistline, front, sides and back.

The following definitions are noted to continue the mutual understanding needed in imparting my proven theories . . . as the same words sometimes conjure up different things to different people.

VOICE: Voice is sound uttered by human beings in song, and is an instrument or medium of expression.

SOUND: Sound is that which is heard. Sound is *tone* or *noise.*

Breathing for singing should not be audible. There should be no noise of intake of breath, nor should gasps of audible inhalation or exhalation of breath be heard. These sounds, which are really unpleasant *noises,* are often louder and more audible than the actual singing, (especially in group or choral singing), and break and impair the melodic line.

When breathing is audible, the process is not only wrong, but also irritates the membranes of the throat and sound box in the skull, and distorts the sound production.

It is mandatory to completely eliminate all extraneous sounds and noises such as the intake of breath before attacking the tone, and the gasping noise after releasing the tone. The only exception to this is the catch-breath, which is studied after the breathing apparatus is perfected.

Do not attack a tone at the same time that you are inhaling.

When starting to sing, visualize preparing the breath as a picture frame which will encompass and frame the tone or phrase.

First take a breath by distending and expanding the diaphragm muscle like a rubber band to its utmost capacity, then wait an instant, suspended before attacking or framing the tone or phrase. Continue singing while the diaphragm muscle is pressing steadily against the outer wall of the body, meanwhile keeping the pelvic muscles raised constantly during the singing. *DO NOT RELAX* these diaphragm and pelvic muscles until an instant *after* the singing ceases. In this way the breath surrounds and frames the singing phrase and there is no audible sound of inhaling or exhaling before or after the singing. *Thus extraneous sounds are automatically eliminated.* The breathing is then noiseless and imperceptible. (See following page)

This is an example to illustrate this point:

Expand the diaphragm muscle;
lift the pelvic muscles.
Wait an instant suspended.

Then sing  Release the tone;

then relax the diaphragm
and the pelvic muscles.

This procedure resembles a picture frame which encompasses and frames the musical phrase, and is actually the basis for the musical natural *legato*.

The following illustrations will demonstrate my meaning:

1

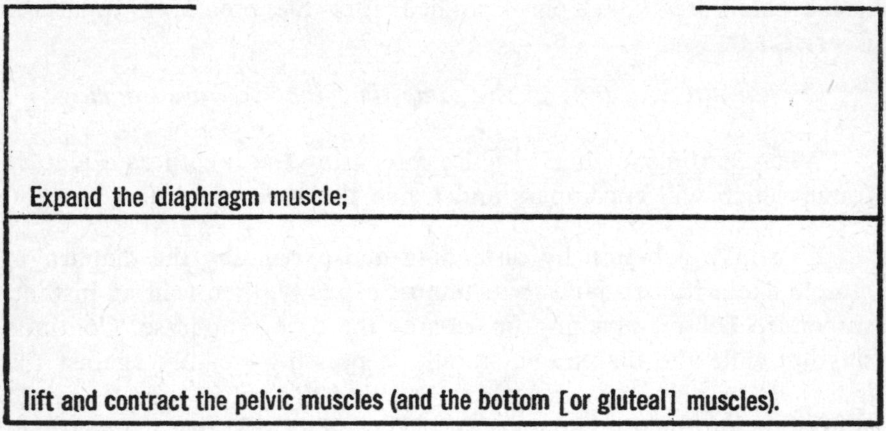

Expand the diaphragm muscle;

lift and contract the pelvic muscles (and the bottom [or gluteal] muscles).

2

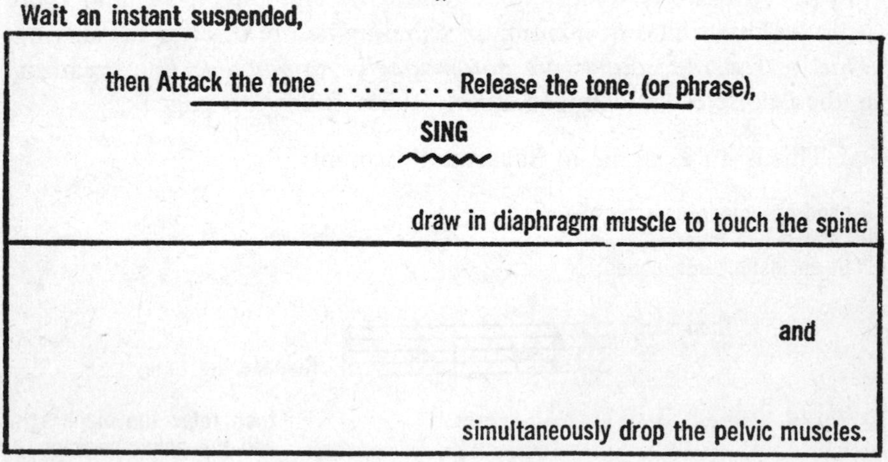

Wait an instant suspended,

then Attack the tone . . . . Release the tone, (or phrase),

SING

draw in diaphragm muscle to touch the spine

and

simultaneously drop the pelvic muscles.

In extreme youth, in fact up to about 21 years of age, the pelvic muscles are so firm by nature that we are almost unaware of their existence and function in singing. At this time we have very little difficulty with these muscles because they are firm and naturally raised. At this age, because of this natural condition, the diaphragm muscle alone seems almost sufficient to keep the placed voice soaring out in all of its glory.

There are two serious, and often disastrous, results which follow the ignoring of the function of the pelvic muscles.

1. The *tremolo,* so often the only fault of an otherwise perfect artist, which is disastrous and serves to nullify the good qualities of voice and artistry.

2. The *faulty pitch* which is the result of the *tremolo.*

It will be wise to pause here to consider the great importance of the pelvic muscles for singing, especially when we look about us and note how many serious singers fall by the wayside enroute to a magnificent career, because of a tremolo, with its accompanying faulty intonation and pitch.

The proper lifting and contraction of the pelvic muscles will eliminate most of the tremolo if the diaphragm and pelvic muscles are employed to release the steady flow of breath through the vocal cords and into the bonal cavities of the head. (The sinuses, nasal passages and eye cavities).

Another cause for a tremolo is pressure on the throat and faulty tongue pressures.

This can be entirely eliminated by perfecting the breathing apparatus and singing single notes with consonant attacks. This regular and correct singing of single tones, always with due regard to proper breathing, will strengthen the throat and neck muscles and vocal apparatus to such a degree that these organs will obey the will of the singer, and completely eliminate the tremolo.

Single tones have proven to be the surest way to build and perfect the vocal apparatus. Choose a middle tone of your voice register and start with the following exercises:

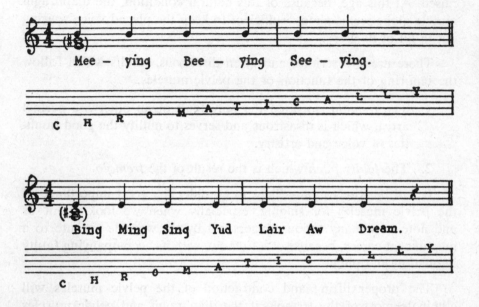

Mee — ying   Bee — ying   See — ying.

Bing   Ming   Sing   Yud   Lair   Aw   Dream.

Practice repeating these long phrases in one breath, attacking each note lovingly, carefully and tenderly, pointing and focusing the flow of breath through the vocal cords and larynx into the head cavities with the focal point between the eyes. (See Fig. 5)

Sing these phrases chromatically up and down the scale, a few tones each way without straining or tiring the voice.

Keep the throat relaxed and open inside, as in yawning.

Every tone should be practiced separately.

Each tone should receive the pitch duration and strength it needs for its own perfection.

Visualize a string of Christmas tree lights and imagine each separate bulb is a tone. Then realize that each tone must sparkle separately in its own place in order to make the entire range of voice even and brilliant, just as each bulb must sparkle to make the range of lights even and brilliant.

This exercise, therefore, is very necessary in training the muscles of the throat, tongue and palate to be flexible, in order that they can function without interfering with the constant, even flow of breath or air which gives us the power to be expressive in singing and achieve this evenness and brilliance.

For it is this column of controlled air pressure into the bonal cavities of the head that forms the crescendos and decrescendos which color and vitalize the voice.

The fine adjustment that enables us to sing an expressive pianissimo requires that our body and voice muscles be so well trained and exercised that we can sing with the least possible pressure of these muscles.

This is the *real secret of beautiful pianissimo singing*. I refer you to the detailed description of the exercises for building muscular control of the diaphragm and pelvic muscles in the preceding chapter.

Never press the throat muscles

The throat must always be relaxed.

This process is the *preservation of the voice; its quality, texture and range.*

CHAPTER IV

VOICE PLACEMENT

Breathing, the foundation stone of singing, must, like the foundation of any structure, be built firmly and securely. I have dealt in great detail with correct breathing in the two previous chapters.

I shall continually refresh the singer with pertinent repetitious reminders of the breathing process, as it constitutes 95 percent of voice production.

Resonance and vibrancy are the next important factors to consider after the breathing apparatus is perfected.

This we call *Voice Placing*.

There are three elements which we must consider in Voice Placing:

1. THE MOTIVATOR — or Breathing Apparatus.

2. THE VIBRATOR — or Vocal Cords and Voice Box (Larynx).

3. THE RESONATOR — or Bonal Cavities — Three resonant walls in the head (sinuses, nasal passages and eyes), our natural Sound Board.

These three elements are indispensable for the production of sound. Corresponding mechanisms are found in all musical instruments, whether wind, reed, stringed or percussion, as well as in the singer.

In instruments these three elements are *unalterable* in their functions as well as in their shapes and sizes.

Each individual has different facial and physical characteristics from the next individual; by the same token each individual has features and cavities of *unalterable shape*.

The facial and physical characteristics of each individual are different from the next individual. The skull cavities and the width and length of the vocal cords as well as the formation of the larynx and pharynx of each individual are different from each other.

Therefore, each singer has a completely individual instrument, which accounts for the variety of quality and texture and range of voices.

This is a unique challenge!

Every singer must explore and perfect an individual new instrument. This is completely and uniquely original and virgin exploration on the part of each singer.

Each singer must then accept the challenge to develop his own instrument to its maximum. To be master of his own instrument and its manifold resources is a worthy goal indeed, and this lofty ambition can be achieved only by self analysis and careful attention to detail.

The singer is so close to his instrument that in the beginning he cannot get a proper perspective, nor can he tell if his tones are properly focused or placed. For this reason it is important to practice with a teacher, coach, accompanist or any other trained listener.

After a time, when correctly placed and focused, the singer's voice sounds to him as if it were detached, outside of his body. Only then can he be his own critic.

If the tone sounds loud inside the singer, it is not placed properly, and will not carry as a full vibrant tone to the audience. Conversely, if the tone is small and resonant inside the singer, then the volume of the tone will sound strong and vital to the audience.

The following definitions are for the meeting of our minds — so that you will comprehend my meaning when I impart my theories to you:

RESONANT: Resounding tone or ring; having the property of increasing sound; intensified and enriched tone; sonorous and vibrant tone.

RESONATING CHAMBERS: Bonal structure of the frontal sinus and sphenoid sinus, nasal passages and eye cavities (the natural sounding board for the voice). (See Fig. 2, page 5)

VIBRANT: Like a resounding drum; voice which adds warmth and beauty to the tone to express changes in emotional intensity. (See Fig. 5, page 41)

Resonance, or vibrancy and sparkle in the tone is what we call a *placed* tone.

The focal point of maximum vibration is usually felt *between the eyes*. Actually, it is when the controlled column of air is propelled upward for singing, that it then vibrates through the vocal cords and adjacent parts, and into the resonating chambers (the vocal sound board) to produce the brilliant, sparkling tone with overtones. These tones which float out and carry throughout an auditorium are called placed tones.

There is a contention, which I consider fallacious: that the sinus cavities and the upper nasal cavity between the eyes exert no influence upon vocalization or vibrant resonance. They contend that the openings of the sinuses are so small and that they are very frequently encroached upon by neighboring parts.

I need only refer the student to the example of the birds, especially canaries, whose cavities are infinitesimal, yet act as tremendous sounding boards for the birds' voices.

Also, it is the great variety in the size and arrangement of the sinuses — sizes and arrangements fixed and established by nature, that makes for the great variety of intensity and brilliance and timbre of voices. This is still another reason why it is so necessary to treat each voice as a new and distinct instrument for exploration.

We must discover and improve our weaknesses, develop and emphasize our advantages, to improve our voice to the best of our ability.

During the process of producing a placed tone, the throat is merely an accessory organ, simply an open passageway for the column of air towards the sound board. Meanwhile, the head, chin, tongue and soft palate should all be completely relaxed.

The placing of the voice is actually the controlled flow of air or breath propelled through the vocal cords and larynx into the resonating cavities, the voice sounding board; then vibrating and floating out, on and with the stream of breath.

All the breath that passes the vocal cords should be converted into and/or transformed into tone or voice. When this is correctly performed, the tone rides out on top of the stream of breath. Otherwise the tone comes out in the middle and is marred and covered, with the air escaping around it. This is what is called a "breathy" tone or voice.

Not a particle of air should be wasted.

The air should produce its equivalent in sound.

Correct humming gives the ideally placed tone, but all people do not hum correctly.

The vowel *e* has nearly the correct resonance in most voices.

The object of the following vocalise is to give to every tone on any syllable or word the same amount of resonance or brilliance as the correct hum at that pitch.

For *Female Voices*: Sing the vowels *a* and *e* on the low notes and *ah* on high notes.

For *Male* Voices: Note that the reverse is true for male singers. Sing *ah* on low tones, *o* in middle, *oo* in highest tones.

The male and female voices have their respective natural forte portions and strength. It is necessary that this be recognized and employed for the best and lasting results. These natural forte portions of the voice must be played up to, in order to preserve them and produce the most desirable results.

The forte portions of the male voice are the middle and the lower portions of the range of the voice.

The female forte portions are the upper-middle and high section of the range of the voice.

This specific phase of voice production has been misunderstood in the past as being what has been misnomered a separate register.

There is but *one register in any voice from end to end of the range*.

The range consists of vibrations from long *to* short which are commonly described as high *to* low, top *to* bottom or, in some cases, chest *to* head tones or vice versa.

In order to clearly understand the ensuing instructions I hereby give my definitions and explanations of *open tones* and *closed or covered tones*.

Open tone means open-throated; physiologically, it means full free passage of the breath *to all the resonating cavities* with a yawning feeling in the throat, and the uvula (the pendulous portion of the soft palate) pointed down.

A closed or covered tone is a concentrated tone; physically produced by narrowing the passageway of the breath by means of the uvula (the pendulous portion of the soft palate). The uvula accomplishes this by bending or reaching inward, thus reducing the area for the passage of the air. Physically, this is demonstrated in singing and accomplished by singing the vowels *EE* or *OO*. This is the reason I have specified using these different vowels to facilitate the proper production of the closed tones in the respective voices.

In view of the respective natural forte portions of the specific voices, the proper application of the breath is necessary for the functioning of the open-throated singing in the middle and lower portions of the male voice. The closing and covering in the higher portions of the range of the male voice is imperative lest he strain and/or impair the vocal apparatus.

A female voice has its forte or strength in the middle and higher portion of the range. Therefore, it is incumbent upon the female singer to produce the open-throated tones in the upper-middle and high sections of her range; and I cannot caution her enough to be sure she closes and/or covers the lower notes in order to preserve the voice and project an even production throughout the entire range of her voice.

Different vowels are specified for the male and female voices in their high and low ranges. The reason for this difference in the two categories is for the purpose of training the voice in the respective high and low ranges so that it may be vibrant and free throughout the entire altitude of its range; and to train the voice in the specific areas for "so-called open" and "so-called closed" or "covered" tones; and to achieve even vibrancy and resonance throughout the range without strain or injury to the vocal cords, because of their specific characteristics.

The natural and most vibrant range of the male singer is the middle and lower range of the voice, which he can open and utilize to its full maximum power without strain or injury to the vocal cords.

The upper (the high notes) range of the male singer, however, is the area of short vibrations which requires special control and care. Therefore, the upper high notes should be covered or closed to avoid straining the vocal cords.

When male high notes are sung, the importance of pointed and focused placement of the voice plus the muscular control of the breath by the diaphragm, pelvic and gluteal muscles come into their most important function to produce and project the required closed or covered high notes of good, resonant quality without injury to the vocal apparatus.

Singing the vowel sounds *EE* and *OO* on the highest notes, and at the same time concentrating a steady and constant flow of breath with special attention to the firm pressure and lifting contraction of the pelvic and gluteal muscles will achieve perfect "covered" or "closed" tones without any strain on the voice.

The reverse is true of the female voice.

In the female voice the most vibrant portion of the range is in the upper-middle and high notes. These tones should be vibrantly brilliant and can be sung fully and freely open (open-throated).

The low tones of the female singer, however, have long vibrations and require concentrated and pointed placement plus the fullest control of the muscular functions of the gluteal, pelvic and diaphragm muscles to cover or close the low tones. This special pressure and lifting contraction of the pelvic and gluteal muscles produces the required effect of vibrancy and resonance in these low tones without straining, and will build and preserve this weakest area of the female voice; because then, the strain is absorbed by the body muscles, and not the vocal organs which are left relaxed and therefore cannot be impaired.

Female voices should sing *EE* or *OO* on the low notes to practice closing these tones.

Therefore, I recommend the singing of these different and opposite vowels in the exercises, scales and vocalises to facilitate the training of the male and female voices to accomplish this end.

The exercises and scales can be interchangeable, but the proper vowel sounds must be applied to suit the specific male or female voice.

Resonance is the *spice* of the voice. Insufficient resonance leaves the voice flat and dull, while too much resonance makes the voice sound harsh. There must be a fine balance and equilibrium of vocal quality and resonant overtones for the best results in singing.

A voice is the main timbre or body quality combined with resonant overtones. The main timbre or body of the voice is your natural God-given gift, and is created solely by the vocal cords vibrating under the influence of breath pressure. The overtones portion of the voice which is the spice, is *created by the singer* when the voice is properly placed and striking the resonating chambers which are hard, bony and cartilaginous substances.

Similarly, the skin cover of a drum, when relaxed, has sound when it is struck, but there is no resonance or carrying quality. However, when the skin cover is drawn tightly over the frame of the drum, and you strike it, you get a resonant vibrating tone. Greater vibration in the drum produces greater resonance and carrying power of the tone.

The vocal range of the singer should be built up carefully by degrees, exercising infinite attention to detail. Therefore, I recommend practicing only fifteen-minute periods at intervals of several hours, resting the speaking voice as well during the intervals you are not singing.

The purity and ease of producing fine high notes in a scale depends entirely upon the manner in which the lower tones leading up to them are sung. If the low tones of a scale or phrase are firmly placed in the resonating cavities and aiming at the focal point between the eyes, it is easier to sing the high notes well.

Unimportant and unaccented tones, grace notes, trills and turns, must be just as carefully and properly *placed* as stressed and accented notes and words.

If the first tones of a phrase, whether high or low, are properly placed, the tones that follow will be correct as well.

The concept of "high" or "low" is arbitrary as applied to sound or voice placement. The Greeks called the sounds "high" and "low" according to the length of the strings on their instruments. This is really the reverse of what we call "high" or "low".

We must admit, for the practical purpose of singing, that we are completely dependent upon our sensations to perfect our instrument, and that we have very little sensation of the physiology involved.

For example: *Pitch* is controlled by varying the *tension* on the vocal cords, and *Volume* is controlled by regulating the air passing through the larynx and adjacent parts. All this is purely academic, because we have no sensation of the vocal cords or larynx. We rely solely upon our hearing and knowledge of music for singing, and tone perception for pitch, and on the control of our breathing apparatus for volume of tone.

Scientific knowledge of the phenomena of the larynx, glottis, pharynx, or vocal cords and soft palate are not absolutely necessary for singing purposes since we do not have any actual *sensation* of their functions. The knowledge of these anatomical parts is purely academic but I recommend that they be studied and understood in order to preserve and properly use them.

The lungs are formed of countless little tubes which receive the air. The lungs are concave and largest at their bases and separated from the abdominal cavity by a convex partition called the diaphragm muscle upon which they rest. When the diaphragm muscle is distended and expanded like a rubber band, the lungs fill with air and are also distended, with most of the air or breath in the lowest or largest area of the lungs which rest upon the diaphragm muscle.

This is also purely academic, as the only sensation we have is that of the diaphragm muscle being distended and contracted. However, it is advantageous to understand and properly employ them, to avoid any strain on the lungs.

The vocal cords are a pair of continuous membrane tissues. The register of the voice is its compass *from end to end* of this pair of membrane tissues (the vocal cords).

Therefore, physiologically, there *cannot* be three so-called registers of the voice, because the vocal cords do not have those separations or demarcations which are implied in speaking of registers.

The one pair of vocal cords have a *continuous* compass which cannot be divided into registers.

Psychologically, it is wrong and often disastrous to think of three registers, and this may be the cause of the "breaks" in voices. It is erroneous to assume that there are three ways of placing the voice; one by the chest, which has no resonance; two, by the mouth which has only soft tissue and does not resound; and third, by the head cavities, (sinuses, nasal passages and eyes), which latter are really the only *"place"* where the voice can resonate.

When the voice is correctly placed and produced, there is only *one register — the entire range —* which should be the same in color-form and quality from its lowest to its highest notes. This procedure relieves the throat and vocal organs of all strain.

Musical instruments have but one continuous register, because they have only one constant sounding board and require one similar technique for playing at any altitude of their range. This is also true of the voice, the most complete and perfect of all instruments because it is the most sensitive and expressive medium for projecting sound or music.

The stroke of the glottis, which is used so often in lieu of attacking a tone, is really the forceful contact of the air hitting against the vocal cords. This explosive *noise* is not only wrong and objectionable on musical and aesthetic grounds, but it is also most injurious to the vocal cords and throat muscles. Furthermore it displaces and distorts the voice.

When you try to sing beyond the extremes of your natural range you are prone to force your vocal apparatus and thereby emit strained tones which sound like bellowing and yelling. When you do so it is really painful to sing and is injurious to your vocal apparatus.

Forcing the voice beyond its natural range and capacity can destroy the quality of vocal tone production, and impair the vocal cords beyond repair.

The tendency to stretch the range beyond the normal capacity with which nature endowed each specific singer is extremely disastrous. This is sometimes indulged in when a low voice attempts to change its "tessitura" for expediency because of the greater opportunities for dramatic effects and because of the greater number of roles written for the high voices. This is a pertinent instance of the fallacy that "farthest fields seem greenest."

In actual fact, a well placed, resonant voice using its natural range, with the proper interpretation of music and text achieves the most dramatic and soul-satisfying effect obtainable.

Pianissimo singing, resonantly and properly produced, has the greatest dramatic appeal and effect upon audiences.

For tone production and voice placing, *slow* singing of the Great Major Scale which follows is the most effective way to insure precision and perfection. More rapid tempos can be applied to other scales later.

Practice slowly and with great care, to *properly place* the first tone of the scale, with special attention to precision of intonation and pitch perception.

GREAT MAJOR SCALE

ADAGIO

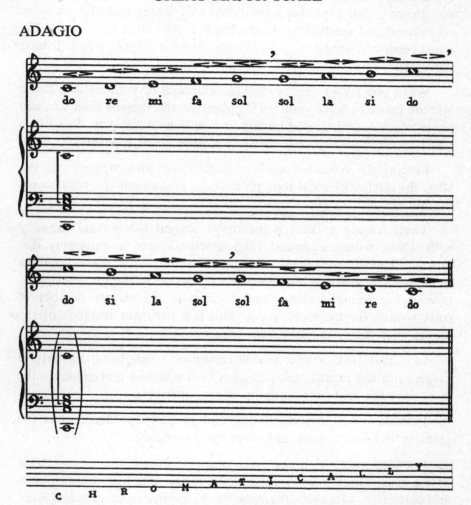

Begin singing each tone gently and softly, then increase the volume quickly, decrease to the lowest possible volume before attacking the following note. Sing chromatically up and down the entire vocal range.

CHAPTER V

DICTION

We have explored and set forth in great detail in the preceding chapters, first, the scientific method of correct breathing; second, the application of the breathing apparatus for singing; and third, voice placement and tone production. All the foregoing is for the purpose of building and perfecting our own instrument to the degree where it will obey our will, talent and individual interpretation and expression.

These prior chapters must be thoroughly and completely understood and assimilated in order to prepare our sound-producing instrument for the next step . . . Diction.

In singing, you have a dual capacity:

1. Interpretation of music and perfect tone production.

2. Reading the poem or text.

Each must be a perfect and complete entity of and by itself. The art of singing is the artful and skillful combining of music and text, not allowing one to interfere with the other, thereby enhancing both mediums.

Diction should not interfere with the breath control or placement of the voice.

Diction should *supplement the voice*. It is solely dependent for its perfection upon the flow of breath and placement of voice in conjunction with the mouth, tongue, teeth, jaws and palate for the formation of the words.

While a song or aria is a musical rendering of a poem or text, it must be remembered that the musical tone (our voice) is of prime importance; and *is the sole purpose of singing*. Therefore, you must never permit your desire for clear articulation to distort or impair or interfere in any way with the natural flow of song or the beauty of your voice.

The following definitions are included to clarify my meanings when referring to these terms:

DICTION: To point out in words; manner of expression in words.

ARTICULATION: Expressing or formulating clearly, distinctly; uniting syllables and words.

PRONUNCIATION: The manner of articulating words: vocal utterance or speech.

SINGING: Elongated and exaggerated speech, which is supported and propelled by the breathing apparatus and resounding into the bonal structure, during which time the tones are shaped and articulated by the mouth, tongue, lips and teeth.

Figure 5

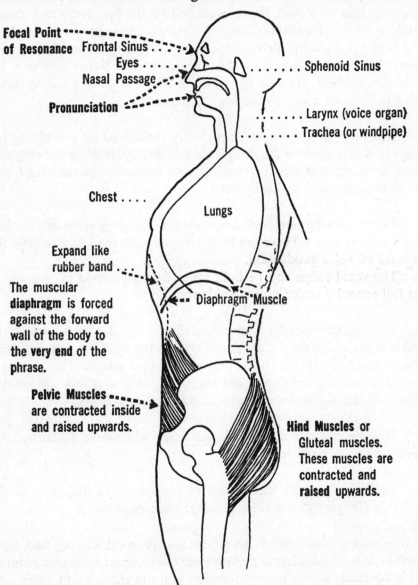

**Focal Point
of Resonance** ---- Frontal Sinus

Eyes ......

Nasal Passage ----

.... Sphenoid Sinus

Pronunciation ----

.... Larynx (voice organ)

.... Trachea (or windpipe)

Chest ....

Lungs

Expand like
rubber band ....

The muscular
diaphragm is forced
against the forward
wall of the body to
the **very end** of the
phrase.

--- Diaphragm Muscle

Pelvic Muscles ----
are contracted inside
and raised upwards.

Hind Muscles or
Gluteal muscles.
These muscles are
contracted and
raised upwards.

Articulation and pronunciation of the text of a song, regardless of the language employed, is accomplished by the lips, teeth and tongue playing upon the stream of musical phrases. These phrases flowing all the way up from the pelvic regions and the diaphragm through the vocal cords and larynx into the cavities of the bonal structure are *like the plucking on the strings of an instrument,* or like soft fingering on the holes of a flute. (See Fig. 5, page 41)

It is only after the voice is perfectly controlled by restraining the too rapid action of the diaphragm muscle and controlling the outgoing flow of breath, that the lips, tongue, teeth and jaws can function freely to pronounce syllables and words.

Every one who can speak has a few good singing notes as a nucleus for a singing voice. These can be developed with the knowledge of the science of voice production.

The vocal range can be built up and strengthened by degrees to its full capacity under proper guidance.

The ringing sound or resonance heard by the singer when the voice is placed in the focal center between the eyes is really the overtones which carry the voice and words into space. This resonant sound is quickly dissipated and only the voice and text are carried along on the air, or breath, and heard by the audience.

This ringing resonance lends the voice and words authority, sincerity, character and personality.

I refer you to the description of resonance as the *spice* of the voice in Chapter IV on voice placing. (See page 34).

So called "emoting" is no substitute for good singing and clear diction and pronunciation and only serves to upset muscular control. This adversely affects tone production and the enunciation suffers.

The mouth and throat form one continuous open passageway.

The proper attack or emission of a tone or word seems to by-pass the throat and mouth organs.

The mouth and throat must have an entirely open, yawning feeling, allowing the unimpeded, controlled flow of breath to aim directly toward the resonating chambers. Meanwhile the tongue, teeth and lips are pronouncing the words while the air or breath is enroute to the focal point for transmission to the audience. (See page 44)

In order to have the throat perfectly open, the jaw must be completely relaxed. It is not necessary that the mouth be open wide. It is the inside of the mouth that should be fully relaxed, as when we quietly yawn.

The singer should feel that the jaw is detached and falling away from the face, as singing is emitted above the nose line, aimed at the focal point between the eyes.

The jaw, teeth, tongue, lips and palate are used only for articulating and pronouncing the text. (See Fig. 6, page 44)

Never press or push the throat in pronouncing. The only place to press is the diaphragm, supporting this with a gentle lifting contraction of the pelvic and gluteal muscles. *This gentle pressure propels the air which projects tone in a slow, steady stream.*

The mouth should only simulate a smile — actually only the cheeks are slightly raised. The "almost" smiling effect is created with the eyes, eyebrows and forehead. Too wide a smile spreads the tone and causes a so-called *"white voice"*, which is unpleasant and should be avoided.

In shaping the passage for the breath, the larynx, tongue, teeth and palate are relaxed and employed to allow the filled lungs to release an even flow of breath (like a punctured balloon) through the vocal cords, to *resonate* and *vibrate* in the *skull* cavities above the *nostrils,* while the *words are formed like the fingering on a stringed or wood instrument.*

Figure 6

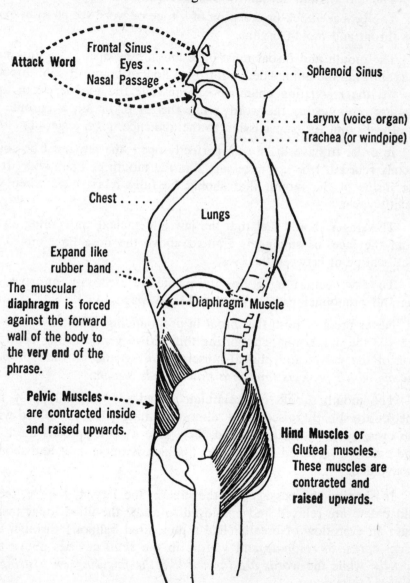

Attack Word

Frontal Sinus . . . . .

Eyes . . . . .

Nasal Passage . . . .

Sphenoid Sinus

Larynx (voice organ)

Trachea (or windpipe)

Chest . . . . .

Lungs

Expand like
rubber band . . . .

The muscular
diaphragm is forced
against the forward
wall of the body to
the **very end** of the
phrase.

Diaphragm Muscle

Pelvic Muscles . . . . .
are contracted inside
and raised upwards.

Hind Muscles or
Gluteal muscles.
These muscles are
contracted and
raised upwards.

The glottis stroke in attacking a word is wrong, and injurious to the throat and voice apparatus as well. There should be no physical sensation or feeling of pressure of any kind upon the throat, inside or outside the throat.

By pretending to put an "H" before a vowel, we get the dramatic effect desired, without the injurious results of using the glottis stroke in singing.

Every word should be sung as though you were in love with it. You will then attack each tone tenderly and lovingly, relying only on the breath pressure for dramatic effects.

You will then sing and pronounce, with complete abandonment of the throat, almost like by-passing or ignoring the throat, which is merely a passageway for the column of air.

The blending of the vowels should likewise take place without any change in the position of the throat during the entire period of singing.

Avoid the exaggerated raising of the head, as it distorts the throat and interferes with the free passage of air or breath.

Tones can be altered and colored by the wise and intelligent manipulation of the cheeks, nostrils, mouth, tongue and palate in various ways to achieve a wide variety of colors and effects that an instrument with constant and immovable parts is incapable of achieving.

Musical intelligence plus the concentration of all your mental and spiritual energy can achieve the full gamut of nuances, inflections, gradations and colors inspired by the text.

The singer must perfect the technical process of singing before he or she can attain perfection as an aesthetic and interpretive artist. Therefore I shall analyze the mouth organs in relation to *diction*.

JAW

The jaw is attached to the skull beneath the temples in front of the ears. By placing your fingers beneath the temples in front of the ears and dropping the jaw, you will find that the space between the skull and jaw widens. While singing, this space must be opened wide. This results in opening the back of the throat and raising the soft palate at the same time.

The jaw, therefore, must be relaxed and dropped away from the face to enlarge the area for the air to flow through. (See exercise below):

Ah—aye-ee—oh—oo ————

Open the throat wide inside as in yawning, and drop the jaw on each word, as follows: *a - e - i - o - u,* pronouncing these vowels on a note in the middle range of your voice. (See mouth shapes page 56)

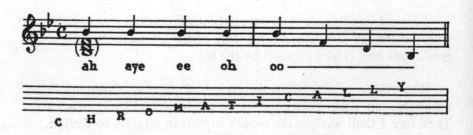

Then later, add consonants to the same vowels as follows:

Lah—Bee—Dah—May ————
Nee—Po—Too—Lah ————
Me—Mo—Mah—Mo—Moo ————
Do—Re—Mi—Fah—Sol-Lah—See—Doh

TONGUE

The tongue should occupy only so much space as it must, without being a hindrance to the tone. Some tongues are too thick, some too thin, some too long, and others too short. These conditions are the challenge to overcome natural shortcomings by making a virtue of a fault, and perfecting your own apparatus.

It is important to realize that the tongue must not rest on the teeth in such a way that might obstruct the flow of tone.

In placing the tip of the tongue against the front teeth, the back of the tongue must be relaxed and flexible. When the tip of the tongue touches the lower front teeth lightly you will note that the sides are raised to form a sort of furrow or trough. This allows the voice free passage to continue flowing out while pronouncing with the tongue. Only in the highest tones, does the tongue remain flat without any furrow.

The tongue must not roll around with its tip during singing. As soon as it has been employed in the pronunciation desired, especially on the consonants *l, n, s, t,* and *z,* in which the tongue is used quickly and sharply and elastically against the upper teeth, it must return to its relaxed position and stay put, to allow the voice to flow out un-hampered.

Exercise for tongue: *ah - o - u -* is a good exercise for the tongue, sung with a yawning effect of the mouth.

Lain - lae—n. lain — touch *l* light to teeth. hold on *ai*, then pronounce n — lain.

TONGUE DRILLS

The following drills should be practised without singing. It may help to watch your tongue in a hand mirror.

Tip of tongue consonants are *d, t, l, n, r, p.*

Back of tongue consonants are *ga, ha, ka.*

1. Touch tip of tongue to upper teeth and then touch lower teeth with tip of tongue and repeat over and over.

2. Hold tip of tongue at edge of lower teeth, then raise and lower middle part of tongue over and over.

3. Hold tip of tongue at edge of teeth, then raise and lower back of tongue and repeat over and over.

Pronounce without singing:

Bahr Behr Bihr Bohr Buhr Bühr Bohr

Bahr Behr Bihr Bohr Buhr Bühr Bohr

Bah Beh Bih Boh Buh Büh Boh

Brah Breh Brih Broh Bruh Brüh Broh

Fd Fd Fd Fd Fd Fddd — Rapidly on one breath

Dah Day Dee Doh Doo — Touch edges of upper and lower teeth. Practice without moving the jaw.

Tah Tay Tee Toh Too — Touch edges of upper and lower teeth. Do not move the jaw while pronouncing.

Rah Ray Ree Roh Roo — Use different degrees of rolling *r* as for Scotch, English or other languages.

Pah Pay Pee Poh Poo — This is a combination for tongue
    and lips.
Trah Tray Tree Troh True
Fah Fay Fee Foh Foo
Lah Lay Lee Loh Loo
Nah Nay Nee Noh Noo

Sing the following single tones:

Pronounce *E* very distinctly after Mi and linger on *ng*

Be sure the *ee* is placed at the bridge of the nose area of the nostrils directly under the eyes.

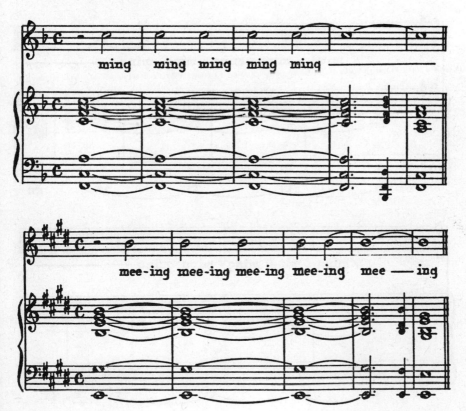

mee-ing   mee-ing mee-ing   mee-ing   mee-ing———

Dee Yee Dee Yee Dee Yee Dee Yee —

Use tongue only — the jaw must be held in same position throughout the exercise.

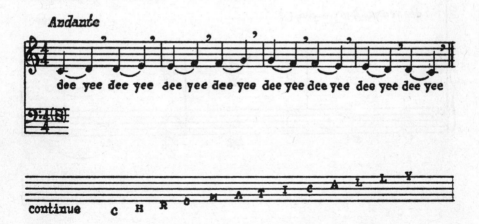

Sing the above chromatically, up and down throughout the entire
vocal range with comfort. Hold the jaw in same position throughout
the entire exercise.

dee yee yee, dee yee yee, (etc.)   yee

dee yee yee, dee yee yee, (etc.)   yee.

CHROMATICALLY

Seeyee   Seeyee

dee — yee — dee — yee — dee yee

CHROMATICALLY

Kayyee   Dayyee

The consonants must be articulated precisely and crisply so as not to interfere with the vowel sounds and the movements of tongue, jaws and mouth, keeping the passageway for the breath constantly free from any obstruction.

LIPS

Every word, vowel and tone can be colored magically by the well-controlled play of the lips, which must be exercised regularly until the muscular power of the lips has been mastered. The same strength, flexibility and elasticity are necessary as in the other vocal organs to pronounce the words of the music without interfering with the constant, steady flow of song.

The following exercises and examples are excellent for lip strengthening: Mah - May - Mee - Moh - Moo.
Pressed — Press — ed — exercise for lips, also jaw and tongue-touching the tongue very lightly against the teeth on *"sd"* sound — Press - ed.

Mine — tongue lingers on upper teeth gently with furrow in tongue for passage of sound.

Bate — late — fate

Laugh — *l* softly against the teeth — *augh* as *uff* with the lips lightly touching teeth and allowing the voice to flow through in a steady stream.

LIP EXERCISES

Mouth Shapes

Mah May Mee Moh Moo ————————

This is a combination of tongue and lip exercises.

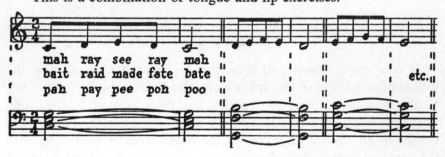

VOWELS

Vowels must be pure and distinct; an *e* should be purely *e* as in
teeth. An *a* should be distinctly *a* as in *ate.* The *i* should sound like the
personal pronoun *I,* the *o* must sound like *blow* and the *u* must sound
like *you* or *oo.*

There must be no empty space or stoppage of tone between words
that break the *legato* of a phrase.

There must never be an escape of breath between vowels; they
must soar out on the controlled stream of breath to form the perfect
legato, a joined melodic line. To make this possible, I recommend use
of the auxiliary sound *y* to connect or join the vowels to each other,
as all vowels must flow into each other. (See exercise)

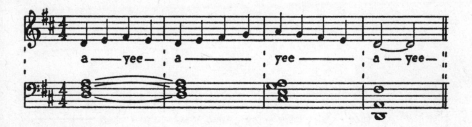

With every change of vowel, there are changes in the position of
all the organs of the throat, the tongue, the larynx and the soft palate
and jaws; therefore, this same exercise serves to exercise all of these
organs at the same time.

The muscular contraction necessary to pronounce these vowels
clearly and properly will help to develop the tongue and jaw to become pliable and elastic, if meanwhile you are careful to fulfill the
fundamentals of proper breathing.

These exercises should be sung only as high or as low as the voice
will allow without straining.

CONSONANTS

The lingual consonants *l, d, t, s, z, r, n, c, y, k, q, x* are prone to interfere with the emission of the tone because of the pull on the tongue.

The root of the tongue is attached to the larynx. In the beginning, the pull disturbs the reflexes and interferes with the steady emission of the voice. The mouth organs must therefore be strengthened to withstand the tension and jerking of the larynx while singing consonants.

The following exercises alternating all consonants and vowels are excellent for the mobility and flexibility and strengthening of the mouth muscles.

Expand diaphragm muscle, raise and hold pelvic muscles, wait an instant suspended, and then sing slowly on single tones, the following:

mee - lah, may - lay, moo - lah, mo - lah ——

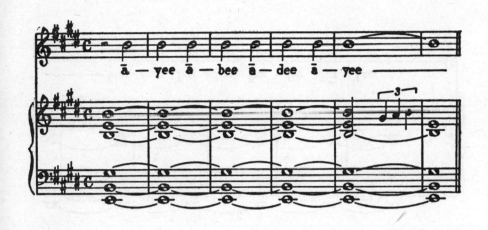

ā — yee ā — bee ā — dee ā — yee ———

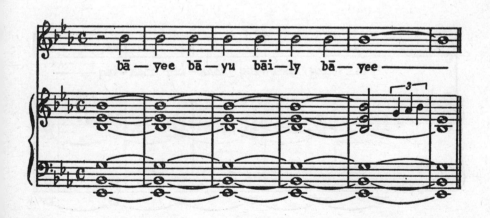

bā — yee bā — yu bāi — ly bā — yee ———

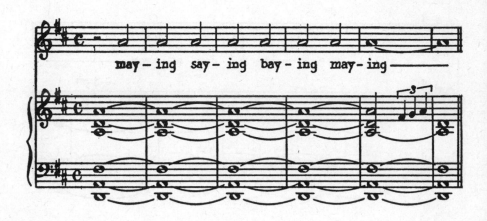

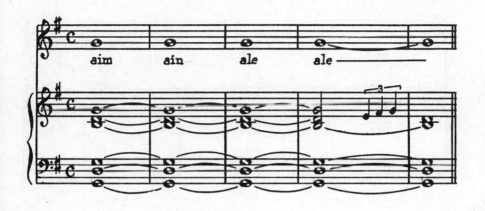

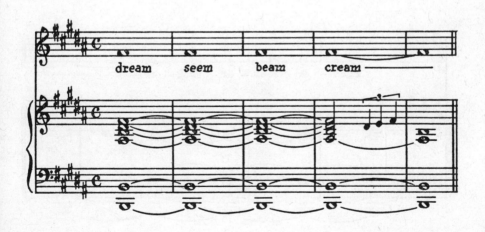

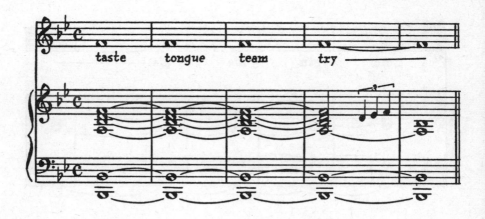

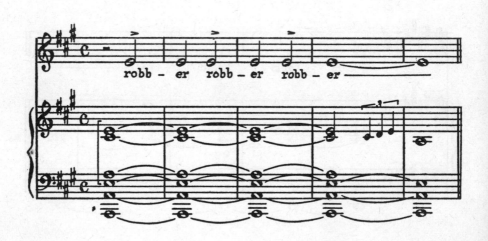

slum – ber num – ber slum – ber———

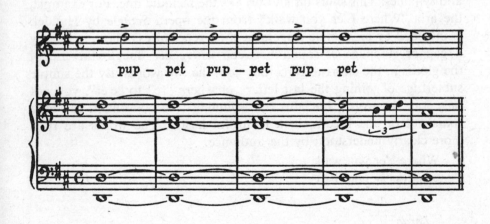

pup – pet pup – pet pup – pet———

The natural legato that we achieve by the control of our own diaphragm and pelvic muscles, (which I have explained thoroughly in a previous chapter), should not be marred by a faulty joining of the words, which allows an instant of space to intervene between words and syllables. This shuts off and breaks the melodic line. For example, the aria "Where E'er you walk" from the opera *Semele* by Handel, is included by most male singers in their repertoires. There is usually a gap or stoppage of sound between *where eër* due to the use of the glottis in the effort to forcefully join the two words. By the simple subterfuge of joining the last letters of whe*re* "re" to "e'er", you not only join the words, but also by "spinning" the consonant, the tone soars out on the breath, in a beautiful legato. The words are then more clearly understood by the audience.

Where e'er you walk

Whe-ree'er you walk

Another example of subterfuge to clarify diction to the audience without impairing the tone occurs in "O, Promise Me" by Reginald de Koven:

Your eyes — you-reyes

And   let   me   sit   be-   side   you,   in   your   eyes

Each song presents its own unique and peculiar problems for proper rendition. These pecularities may arise out of a specific combination of words in conjunction with the musical requirements. In some cases a given word may offer specific problems within a particular vocal range of the voice.

Often composers do not take into consideration the problems of voice production when they create. Therefore, each song must of necessity be thoroughly studied to fit your own singing instrument, so that your specific voice will be displayed at its best.

CHAPTER VI

VOCALISES AND SCALES

The voice is a very delicate instrument which cannot be replaced or repaired. That is why I stress that *not one tone be sung thoughtlessly or carelessly,* and why I recommend *singing vocal exercises for short periods only, at regular intervals.*

The singer's goal should be to sing with perfect facility from one end of the voice range to the other, singing all tones clearly and resonantly and with plenty of power in reserve.

Each tone of the scale must sound the same in quality and brilliance and be as beautiful as the preceding and following tones.

The purpose of practicing vocalises and scales is to build up the strength of the vocal cords and apparatus; to improve the voice and add to its range; to minimize weaknesses and emphasize advantages and natural gifts.

Exercises and scales *are no substitute* for careful voice building but are a necessary and important adjunct for strengthening and building the voice. Exercises are also sung for the purpose of fixing the intonation and pitch, while securing the steady flow of tone via the diaphragm and pelvic muscles.

66

Acquiring a fine precision of pitch and a firm legato are also included in the regular and faithful application to exercises and scales. Each exercise and scale should be sung as carefully as any song or aria. Each note must retain the same placement of voice and the same intensity of resonance from beginning to end; attacking the first tone an instant after the breath (breathing apparatus) is firm, then singing the scale with maximum care and beauty of tone until the last note is finished; then collapsing the diaphragm and pelvic and gluteal muscles.

This is where all the knowledge that you have acquired about breathing, muscular control and voice placement (discussed previously in the second, third and fourth chapters) comes into play.

Before singing any exercise, scale, or tone, *be sure* that your body is completely relaxed and "limbered up"; applying all the instructions absorbed from the previous chapters. Then you may properly attack and sing the ensuing scales without strain. As in an athlete the "limbering up" of the muscles causes the blood to flow to exercised muscles. In the vernacular of baseball, it is the "warming up" that is, simply preparing the muscles of the body to perform what the mind commands and to obey without stress or strain.

Vocalises must be sung only as high or as low as the voice can comfortably reach without strain. After you arrive at a comfortable basis of a few middle range notes, you should then work towards the high and low extremes of your vocal range.

With faithful, regular application and steady purpose you will find that your range will increase its compass, slowly, but surely. In addition, the voice grows more beautiful in quality and becomes more flexible in singing either modern dissonant intervals or florid coloratura pyrotechnics.

Vocalises and scales sung only on vowels tend to carelessness of focal direction and ultimate strain on the vocal cords and throat muscles. I therefore call your attention to the consonants accompanying the scales and exercises.

I suggest alternating vowel attacks with consonant attacks; the consonants to be uttered at the outermost tip of the tongue, clearly, quickly and distinctly, so as not to interrupt the purity of the vocal line (legato) and always with due regard to pitch, line, intonation, color and steadiness.

At this time I would like to comment upon the *tremolo* which so often is the only fault some singers have and which immediately detracts from their stature as artists. This is another elusive obvious, because its cause and correction are so basic and simple.

The tremolo has many ramifications, as it produces uncertain pitch perception and causes the singer, in an effort to steady the tone, to push with the vocal cords and produce so-called "sharp" intonations or "flat" intonations.

The tremolo also interferes with interpretation. Because a note or a word that should be authoritative and firm sounds tremulous and faulty in pitch. Thus, the tremolo serves to nullify the virtues of a beautiful voice and fine artistry to the ears of critics and audiences.

You will note my repetitious reference to the *pelvic* and *gluteal muscles*. These are the muscles we feel when we are seated and press down upon.

These *pelvic* and *gluteal muscles* should be raised or elevated inside the body and held firmly throughout the entire singing phrase. This will eliminate the tremolo, on condition that the tone is also perfectly placed, and the remainder of the breathing apparatus (the diaphragm) is perfectly controlled at the same time.

Even if, and especially when, the singer becomes nervous before an audience, this same *pelvic* raising and contracting with the diaphragm control will correct any tendency to tremolo and the nervousness then will not be perceptible to the audience.

This accentuates the need for the breathing exercises that I have described at great length, and also points up their basic importance.

If I may reiterate, and I cannot repeat it often enough, that *a tremolo can undo your singing career!* Therefore, I must stress again the importance of the practice of the breathing exercises over and over throughout your entire singing career.

SCALES, VOCALISES AND EXERCISES

There are many books, currently available, of scales and exercises for making the voice flexible, which the student, especially a beginner, may study under the guidance of a teacher, with great benefit to himself or herself.

I am, however, including in this handbook some especially important examples of exercises and scales that have proven their worth beyond any doubt in my years of experience.

There are *separate* categories for male and female voices. I admonish you to pay special attention to the difference and distinction in the vowel sounds that are designed to facilitate the placement of the voices while singing these exercises and scales. In some cases the scales and exercises may be similar and interchangeable for both male and female voices. But they must be sung on *different* vowels for each type of voice according to their respective categories. (See page 31)

I have stressed the purpose of each individual scale, and also indicated the manner in which each scale should be sung. If faithfully and carefully followed, always with due regard to the breathing procedure and placement of the voice at the resonating focal point, (which I have explained and described in great detail in previous chapters), these exercises will result in ultimate accomplishment, with its resultant perfection of your singing voice.

Concentrate first upon acquiring an easy, relaxed and persuasive attitude of the body before starting to vocalize. Be sure that your posture is correct, that your head is held normally (not raised, uncomfortable or distorted), that your arms dangle relaxedly, that you can sway easily upon the balls of your feet.

Only then, when you are sure of your posture and breathing apparatus, do you proceed to vocalize, practicing slowly and carefully, (with great attention to all the foregoing details), and with greater attention to intonation, quality, pitch and placement.

FEMALE VOICES

In view of the difference in the forte portions of voices between male and female singers, these vocalises are given as examples to train and strengthen the natural vocal production without strain, to produce the best possible result.

This procedure will also equalize the voice. As a reminder of the lengthy explanation in Chapter IV, the forte portion of the female voice is the upper-middle and high range, and the forte portion of the male singer is the middle and low range of the voice.

Bearing this in mind, the following exercise serves to point up the focal resonating area. It should be sung chromatically, a few notes above and below the middle range of the voice. Press lips crisply on *M*, follow quickly with double *"e e"* sound, then finish by exaggerating the auxiliary *Y*, ying. This brings out what I referred to in a previous chapter relating to the sound being "outside the body" . . . detached from the body.

The *yng* sound seems to hit the upper wall of the nostrils near the eyes when sung correctly.

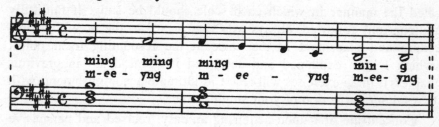

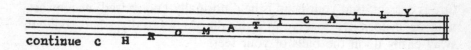

continue CHROMATICALLY

The following scales are divided into two catagories, for male voices and female voices.

FOR FEMALE VOICES

Expand the diaphragm — raise the pelvic muscles — wait an instant suspended — then press diaphragm muscle in strong "panting" action on each staccato note.

Chromatic scales for precision of intonation.

Alternate vowels and consonants. Make sure of an even tempo from start to finish to cultivate rhythmic feeling.

The *yng* sound seems to hit the upper wall of nostrils near the eyes, when sung correctly. ·

The following scale equalizes the voice quality throughout the middle vocal range.

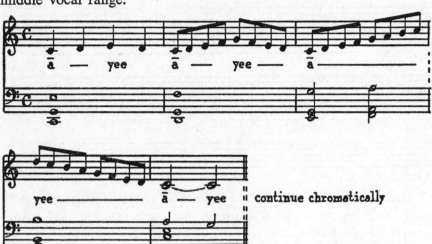

The auxilliary *y* exercises the tongue in the foregoing scale.
The interrupted arpeggio prevents carelessness in voice placing.

The momentum which carries the voice to the octave above is suddenly interrupted and requires concentration to place the decending and ascending tones that follow. This prevents carelessness as in regular arpeggios.

Legato and staccato arpeggios flex the diaphragm muscle.

This arpeggio is sung first legato and repeated staccato, with special care to *press* the *diaphragm for each staccato and avoid pressure on the throat.*

Major scale for intonation, pitch and quality.

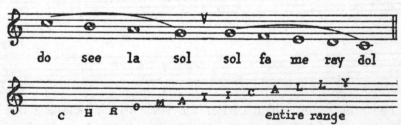

This scale must be sung very slowly and carefully. It is useful not only for sustaining the diaphragm and pelvic muscles, but also for tone placement and intonation.

Cadenza with proper female vowel, for flexibility and jaw exercise.

dee - - - - - - yaw - - - - - - dee - yee

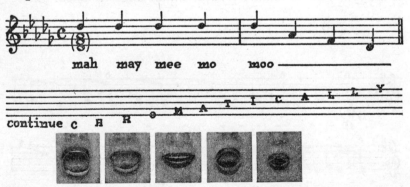

entire range of voice
without straining.

Sing rapidly and evenly except for a slight accent after the bar lines, with a yawning feeling in the mouth on the higher notes on *Yaw*.

Consonant precision, plus mouth shapes for exercises of jaw and lips.

mah may mee mo moo

This exercise is excellent for strengthening the jaws while opening the inside of the mouth in the various shapes; also closing the lips on *M* consonants distinctly.

HALF-TONE TRILL AND WHOLE-TONE TRILLS

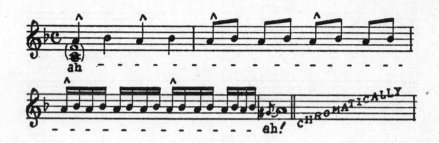

In trilling, the natural tendency is to stress the higher note of the trill. However, the higher note has a more rapid vibration then the lower note which makes it sound slightly louder; therefore, in order to equalize the tones and acquire an even trill, it is necessary to practice both the half-tone trill and the whole-tone trill with *a slight accent on the first lower accent note*. The result will be that both notes are produced to sound equal in volume and brilliance.

Octaves for attack practice.

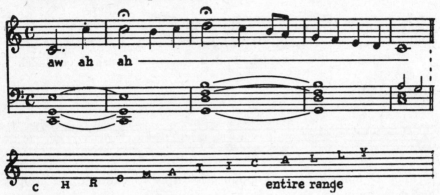

Sing the first note legato. Attack the octave above staccato. Then finish legato.

Exercise for agility and intonation.

Intonation is the chief object of this exercise in addition to the flexibility it develops. This should be sung in full voice (but not too loud) and then repeated in pianissimo (softly).

Staccato and legato exercises and jaw exercises on *D* consonant.

The *D* consonant is pronounced crisply to exercise the tongue and jaw, singing on the vowels as long as possible within their allotted span. Note the combination of legato and staccato.

Arpeggio for agility and flexibility.

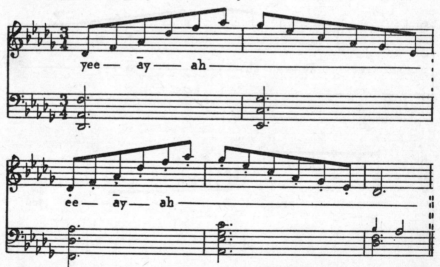

This should be sung full voice ... first part legato and then repeated in staccato. Repeat again softly (or mezzo-voce), being sure to have the same intensity of resonant vibration in the pianissimo (soft singing).

Intervals for intonation and attack.

This should be sung within the range of the voice without straining, attacking distinctly and clearly, without slurring or scooping the tones.

MALE VOICES

Single tone scale for establishing and fixing pitch and intonation.

Sing these vowels carefully, then apply the words *Ming ming ming ming ming* to the same notes. Press lips crisply on *M*, follow quickly with double *ee* sound; finish on *yng — mee-yng*. This serves to separate the tone from the body, sounding detached or outside the body (which I described in a previous chapter). The *yng* sound seems to hit the upper wall of the nostrils near the eyes, when sung correctly.

Five note exercise for flexibility and jaw and lip exercise.

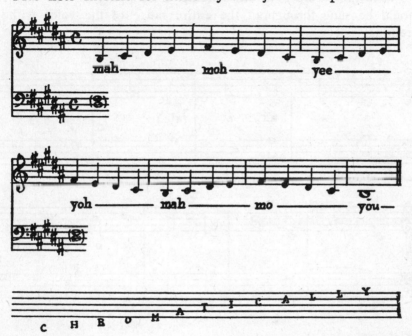

This exercise includes the various intervals and is useful for precision of attack and practice for the legato singing.

For precision of intonation.

This exercise includes the various intervals and is useful for precision of intonation.

Take great care to avoid slurring or scooping into tones. This should be sung throughout the entire range of the voice without straining.

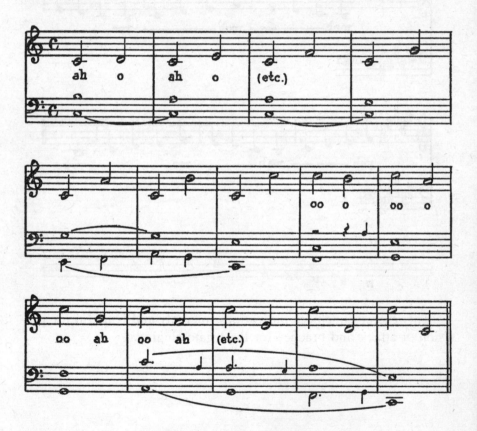

Alternate vowels and consonants. When you sing make sure of an even tempo from start to finish.

For Baritone and Basses

For Tenors

For High Baritones

For Tenors

For Tenors

Excellent for flexibility.

yaw ——— yoo ——— yaw ——— yoo ——— yah —

CHROMATICALLY

Press diaphragm out on each staccato tone.

yaw yee yoh ——————— yee ——————— yaw

CHAPTER VII

INTERPRETATION OF
SONGS AND MUSIC

It is largely talent plus intelligent and painstaking practice and work that enables one to perfect the art of singing.

Work does not mean unguided or unsupervised singing of scales and vocalises; nothing could be more harmful to the vocal organs. Work to the true or potential artist means intelligent direction under the proper guidance of a teacher or coach; painstaking study and practice, and an infinite capacity for detail.

Physically speaking, each individual is endowed by nature, with the same vocal and physical parts and organs in various degrees of perfection.

The great artists are those who have taken pains to perfect their physical parts and vocal apparatus to their utmost capacity, so that they will be free from any worry physically and can devote their entire talent and attention to the interpretation, not only of the music of the song, but also the poem or text that inspired the music.

Our reservoir of power is, of course, basically our breathing apparatus, which is the motive power of the physical act of singing. Therefore, it might be expedient and useful to review and touch lightly upon this subject of breathing, which I have explained in such great detail in previous chapters.

This manner of breathing is really imperceptible to the audience. This is because the posture of the shoulders drawn back, and the raised chest remains stationary, while the expanded diaphragm and raised pelvic muscles inside the body, constitute the principle agents for sustaining the column of air in the lungs; while the air is slowly released and transformed into sound or voice.

This manner of breathing is also the most effective way of getting the lungs *full of air,* and the most effective control of the *emission of air* so that every particle of air can be converted and/or transformed into voice, *upon which we put words.*

This preparation of the diaphragm and pelvic muscles supplies plenty of breath for the completion of any sentence, with usually ample breath in reserve, after the artistic journey of music and text.

This exhibition of ample reserve breath, gives the rendition of a song or aria great authority and confidence which communicates itself to the audience; and as this breathing is imperceptible to the audience, it gives the appearance of *effortless singing, which indeed it is!*

This breathing gives your audience the impression that there is no limit to your resources!

Art begins only where technique ends; therefore, I repeat, that the body and vocal instrument must be perfected in order to give the maximum expression to the *music, text and mood* of the song or aria, whether modern nuances or florid pyrotechnics and coloratura singing are required.

In the process of interpretation of songs, the technique of breathing and voice production should be applied consciously and deliberately.

A prevailing opinion about technique is "once you have learned it, forget it." This is a destructive fallacy that does not hold true for a successful singing career. I contend that once you have mastered the techniques of scientific breathing and singing you must *never forget them.*

Technique should not be forgotten but should become so automatic that it obeys the will of the singer. Not a note should be sung without deliberately and consciously utilizing the diaphragm and pelvic muscles for breathing and the head cavities (sinuses, eyes and nasal resonating walls) for tone placement with its resonance and overtones.

In singing art songs of vocal literature, we are usually confronted with comparatively simple tasks, especially when the song is in the language which inspired the composer. Then the accent beat of the music is also the accent syllable of the word. This is what is known as a true wedding or marriage of music and words.

I advise whoever essays to learn a song to begin by reading the words and realizing their full meaning and power.

However, the approach to the study of a song's first step is optional, depending upon the individual's own aptitude and inclination. To some it is simpler and easier to study the music first, then the text and later join the two in practice. To others it may be the reverse.

But no matter how you decide to study the song, there is still another and more elusive factor to consider — and that is the soul and spirit which the composer not only felt and was moved by when composing the song, but hopes that you will interpret and convey to your audience.

The overall prevailing *mood* of the song must be grasped, because this is the elusive factor which lends the song color.

Some songs and arias conjure up a variety of colors, running the gamut from lightness and gaiety to seriousness, and even tragedy. Other songs are humorous or narrative; poetic or lofty; earthy or witty; sacred or sentimental; or a combination of moods and a variety of colors.

The capturing of this elusive quality, which we call *mood*, is one of the greatest achievements in interpreting songs and arias, since it is not dependent upon gestures or stage tricks, but is solely dependent upon *your* inner perception and sympathetic understanding of the text in combination with the music which the text inspired.

This treatise is essentially about the science and art of voice production and this chapter is devoted to interpretation. Therefore, I am assuming that the study of sight singing and music has preceded the serious training which is now to be embarked upon.

It is hardly necessary to dwell upon the immense advantages those individuals possess who have learned sight-singing and music prior to this study of singing and the analysis of song interpretations.

There are three factors involved in preparing a song or aria:

1. Musical importance and interpretation (composer's meaning)

2. Text and grammatical importance and interpretation (poetic meaning)

3. Vocal quality and voice production (personality of singer)

An essential feature of music, as of poetry, is the constant recurrence at regular intervals of an accented sound. The metric accent measures time into fragments of equal length. It is unnecessary to express this accent in poetry because the pronunciation of the words supplies it. In music, however, in order that no mistake be made, a vertical line is placed before the sound to be accented. These vertical lines, called bars, divide the music into measures.

A song is, of course, studied with due regard to the wedding of music and text, and to making the most of the relation of one to the other, musically and histrionically.

In the study of "O Sleep, Why Dost Thou Leave Me" from the opera *Semele* by Handel, we shall consider the first phrase:

oh ———————————————————————— sleep

Handel.

The classical composer, Handel, evidently wanted the first word attacked quietly and unobtrusively; therefore, he placed the first word (*O*) on the second, unaccented and unimportant beat of the measure. He then continued the melody only to return to the same note and word (Bar 2) on the first accented beat. This gives it its pulse and rhythm; after which he continues the musical phrase and concludes on the word *Sleep* (Bar 3) also on the accented beat. By singing the text musically correct, you then need only to project your imagination into the *soul and spirit* of the text. Be sure, in this phrase, to hold *Slee*— for two beats, pronouncing *p* at the very end of the second beat, distinctly *Slee-p*.

In "None But the Lonely Heart" by Tchaikowsky:

Nur   wer   die   Sehn —   sucht   kennt

"Nur Wer Die Sehnsucht Kennt" by Tchaikowsky
Nur is on the first accent beat (Bar 1); so also is *Sehn* (Bar 2) — the accented part of *"sensucht"*. This beautiful song is another example of an artistic and effective joining of words and music.

"Oh, Promise Me", by Reginald De Koven

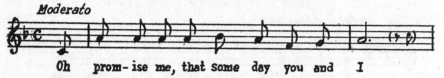

Oh   prom-ise me, that some day you and   I

In "Oh, Promise Me" by Reginald De Koven the accent beats are on *prom* (Bar 1) — the first syllable of *promise* — and *I* (upbeat) which when sung in this manner will be correct musically, and tells you immediately what the composer intended. The *I* should be held until the end of the three beats (Bar 2).

I shall take this opportunity to stress the importance of singing the vowel sounds as long as possible within their time allotment; touching distinctly and lightly on the consonants; spinning the consonants so that they flow through the furrowed tongue which permits the constantly continuing flow of sound.

We shall now consider the Waltz Song from Franz Lehar's *The Merry Widow*, which is written in three-quarter time (3/4 meter).

You will note that the best effect is obtained by accenting definately the first beat of *every other bar*. Then you will get a better waltz feeling than accenting the first beat of each bar. This is the "exception that proves the rule."

The Merry Widow by Franz Lehar.

Tho'   I   say   not   what I   may not let you hear.

The accents are after *every other* bar as noted: *Though, what, let,* and *hear.*

In French songs, we have the problem of the language to consider. In the French language most of the syllables have an equal amount of stress and there is little opportunity for accent. It is therefore more important than ever to regard the composer's musical wishes.

"Elegy" by Massenet

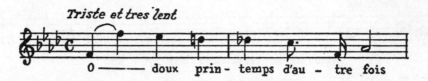

Triste et tres lent

O ———— doux prin - temps d'au - tre fois

In Massenet's "Elegy," the *O*, started on the accent beat (Bar 1), is on the low *F* which indicates that Massenet wanted the high *F* note following on the second beat to be sung unobtrusively and unaccented, although the normal tendency in singing is to bring out and give more importance to high notes. The effect is startling and thrilling.

The purity and beauty and ease of singing the high notes of a phrase are dependent upon the manner in which the preceding lower tones leading up to the higher notes are placed and sung.

For instance, in "Rejoice Greatly" from *The Messiah* by Handel:

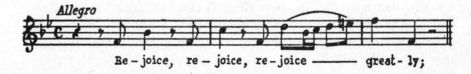

Allegro

Re - joice, re - joice, re - joice ———— great - ly;

when the *Re* on *F* (Bar 1) is placed properly — the *joice* falls into place easily. The first *rejoice* is quiet and unaccented; the second *re* must be unaccented but placed carefully in order to sing *joice* on the following accent beat of the music (Bar 2); the third *rejoice* is also unaccented, continuing quietly until the third bar; then accent the first syllable *great* of *greatly*.

These portions of songs are merely examples of how to approach the interpretation of songs. These few examples, with the guidance of a teacher or coach, may be used as a guide to analyze and interpret any song you wish.

To facilitate the preparation of a song, it is vitally important that you first memorize the words and music. After you have committed both the text and music to memory, you can more readily digest the subtle inner meaning of the song.

After the song is thoroughly explored and understood from the musical standpoint, and your breathing and vocal apparatus obeys your will automatically, you can then sing freely and interpret your song in such a manner that will make it distinctly your own style whereby *your own personality shines through.*

This explains why the same song, sung by different artists always seems different, because of the distinction in personality and style of each singer.

CHAPTER VIII

SONG RECITAL

In the concert recital, the singer has a much more difficult task than in opera or the oratorio, because he or she must hold the attention of the audience without the assistance of histrionics, costumes or scenery.

Only by his or her own artistry, personality, charm and appearance, in conjunction with the artist's vocal ability and interpretive power does the singer essay to interest and thrill the audience.

The program offered must serve to bring out these qualities of the singer to their maximum degree, because the *singer stands alone upon the stage!*

There is a fitness in the choice of songs for a concert program, which should be as carefully planned as an edifice.

First, there should be laid down a firm foundation, as for the edifice, likewise for the voice; to present your gift of song to your audience in proper sequence.

Heretofore it has been a successful practice to begin with classics of early periods of music, usually sustained in tone, dignified and beautiful to the listening audience, while at the same time rewarding to the singer.

Bear in mind that the first song not only creates the communion between the artist and audience, but also serves the purpose of steadying the finely attuned nervous system of the singer.

Nervousness of a singer before a performance is not unusual.

Do not despair! It is a feeling common to all performers, singers, speakers, dancers and athletes as well; and to me nervousness is an indication of fine sensibilities and can be utilized to serve the singer's purposes musically and dramatically.

I shall here refer you to the previous chapters with special attention and emphasis upon the use of the pelvic and gluteal muscles, which, when used properly, serves to make the nervousness imperceptible to the audience; meanwhile keeping the voice firm and soaring out in great steadiness of tone.

Upon this firm foundation should be built a graceful and interesting structure with a few potent points borne in mind to create and hold the "entente cordiale" between the singer and audience and retain the interest of the audience to the end of the concert.

There is of course, no end to the variety of music that may be included in framing or building your program, and there are several vital points to take into account, such as their suitability to your vocal apparatus, your flexibility of vocal achievement, the gender of the songs, the key signature of the songs in their relation to the preceding and following songs. Also the moods of the songs, with regard to emotion, drama, style, period, language and/or composer are to be considered.

It might help to bear in mind the movements of a Symphony, which usually consists of four movements contrasted in mood and tempo.

There should be an artistic entity in a program made of a variety of colors and moods and tempo with plenty of opportunity to display technique and flexibility.

All singers from the coloratura soprano on down to the lowest bass voice should be able to sing flexible, pyrotechnical arias and songs!

The whole concert should be cohesive, as well as interesting, with an easy natural and progressive sequence toward your final goal, which is the overall impression you wish to leave with your audience.

This ultimate goal should not deter you for an instant from *singing each song* as though it were the only song on your program; projecting into each song your maximum of vocal accomplishment, musical interpretation as well as poetic insight into the diction and style.

The greatest care should be taken in choosing the songs that make up each group, so that they contrast well in musical key, in mood, in character and style, even though they might be written by the same composer, or by various composers of a certain similar language or country or period.

In considering songs or arias, it is also supremely important to note the gender of the song, as it is awkward for a woman to sing sentiments meant for a man and vice versa.

Operatic arias are no problem because they are clearly defined and indicated as male or female arias — with the exception of those arias written in the early eighteenth century; for example, the title role of *Orpheus* by Gluck, and Urbino from Meyerbeer's *Les Hugenots* and even later, Siebel in *Faust* by Gounod, when the curious musical fashion prevailed of assigning contraltos and mezzo-sopranos to male roles. In recent times Richard Strauss also assigned a male role to a contralto, Octavian in *Die Rosenkavalier*.

Oratorios are also clearly defined as to their gender, with possibly a few airs that can be termed neuter in gender and can be sung effectively by either man or woman, such as "Oh, rest in the Lord" from the *"Elijah,"* although I feel that Mendelssohn purposely assigned this aria to the female voice with an awareness of the differences of the male and female voices in the higher notes.

In the enormous repertoire of song literature, (exclusive of opera and oratorios), there is seldom anything except the character of the words to indicate the sex intended by the composer and poet. Therefore, it behooves you to ponder deeply and seriously each song in order to portray the musical and poetical message with full sympathy for and understanding of the music and text of each song.

Program Example:

A first group may conceivably consist of early classics like Handel, Haydn, Mozart, Bach, Beethoven or Gluck.

A second group may be chosen from the Romantics: Schubert, Schumann, Brahms, etc.

A third group might be French songs of early vintage or Debussy, Duparc, Ravel and countless others.

Another group might be a Song Cycle, a Spanish group, or a group of an individual composer with special attention to its variety in mood, color, drama and tempos. A florid pyrotechnical operatic aria may be sung between groups which will display your vocal wares and abilities to your public.

A last group might be one of contemporary composers, and/or English and American songs, or folk songs.

You have unlimited latitude in your choice of songs, dependent upon the extent of your repertoire.

The singer must cultivate the habit of preparedness; of thoroughly studying and mastering the music and text and mood of the song until it becomes his own.

Avoid imitation of another singer's rendition of the same song or the affectation of another singer's mannerisms. Certain external effects which are suitable and charming in one individual may not be appropriate in another individual. Therefore, I urge that you delve deeply into the *inner perception* of the song or aria and let your own personality shine through.

Do not depend upon the inspiration at the moment of singing to supply your needs. You must be thoroughly prepared and inspired before the recital, so that *your personality will be welded with the song.*

Personality is the sum total of distinctive attributes and individual qualities considered collectively, as likely to impress others.

It is this elusive quality we call *personality* which is finally the most valuable asset to the singer and which can be developed by sheer projection of your character and being.

Personality may be cultivated to a certain extent, but in the last analysis, it is the *Real You.*

Charm is another elusive quality invaluable to a singer. Charm is the ability to fascinate your audience; to enchant and delight them with your personal allure and the magic of your personality.

Charm can be cultivated!

My final admonition to the singer is to caution you to express and feel genuine affection and love for your audience by the persuasive attitude of your body and face.

This love communicates itself to your audience and they return the affection to help you make a success of *Your Song Recital.* "Love begets Love."

CHAPTER IX

GRAND OPERA

Every ambitious student of singing envisions a concert or opera career as his or her goal. Often with the added careers of record making, television performances, radio engagements and motion picture assigments in the background as hopeful possibilities.

The inner urge that animates your desire to be a great artist will lead you to accept and grasp every aid to achieve that end, which should include a thorough study of histrionics (acting technique) and languages.

To reach your goal and accomplish your aim is not via the path of least resistance. The inner impulse to press on to succeed in a career is a great factor and will lead you to improve your equipment vocally, physically, histrionically, and linguistically. All of these must be mastered to the fullest extent of your ability.

You cannot acquire these necessary accomplishments vicariously; this entails dedicated work mentally, vocally and physically.

You, in the last analysis, must be your own harshest critic.

"I do but sing because I must," wrote the poet, Tennyson.

With world conditions constantly changing, America stands as the strong citadel of the world's music.

Undoubtedly one of the principal causes of increased interest in music and singing in America is the development of music in colleges, universities and high schools. The importance of this influence and effect upon our culture has been stressed by the inclusion of music as an essential part of the curriculum.

Colleges and universities are currently producing operas on a progressively grand scale, giving serious and talented students opportunities to try their wings before audiences. In former years, it was almost mandatory that singers go to Europe to get their experience, singing before audiences in the small town opera houses of Europe.

This procedure is still available, of course, but not absolutely necessary, due to our constantly, although slowly, increasing appreciation of our native talent.

I urge groups of mixed voices in our colleges and universities to show initiative and gather weekly, or at least at regular intervals (extra curricular) to sing together, and eventually to sing and act opera and oratorios for sheer joy as well as education. In the same way instrumentalists (even professionals in symphony orchestras) meet regularly for the pleasure and satisfaction of playing chamber music and rarely heard scores.

Why can't we have Intercollegiate Opera and Concerts in the same way that we have Intercollegiate Football and Track meets!

There are many useful and practical suggestions that can help smooth an otherwise rugged pathway along the musical road to opera, and I shall continue a compilation of the major necessities.

Almost equal to possession of a fine voice to a singer is the ability to do your prescribed task quietly, systematically, and without giving trouble to the management of the opera. The so-called temperament attributed to singers should be reserved for, and confined to, your voice and the interpretation of the role, and not as a display of bad temper.

Versatility is also a very important asset in singing and portraying operatic characters, but care must be taken not to displace the vocal apparatus in an effort to sing a role unsuited to you vocally.

Do not attempt to be versatile at the expense of your voice.

An added reminder here: never, never forget that air is the element of sound (your voice) and that your *breathing apparatus,* (the muscular control of the pelvic and diaphragm muscles pumping air up through the vocal cords and into the bonal, resonating head cavities), *are the prime factors to master* before proceeding with the preparation and study of operatic roles.

The voice must be beautiful, first, last and always! No matter what position or posture you may be called upon to assume or portray.

I urge very strongly that most of your study should be mental; memorizing the music, words and character of the role before you attempt to sing the opera. You will then find, that you will be more careful to use your breathing and vocal apparatus with the special care and respect that they deserve. Especially, if you wish to *maintain and retain* the beauty and freshness of your voice throughout your chosen career.

Preparedness is another asset for a potential operatic aritist that cannot be over-emphasized. *Knowing* thoroughly the *roles that suit your temperament* in the standard repertoire of opera may be the means of launching you, as it has for many others in the past, upon a career of your chosen profession.

Many well known artists of the past were called upon to sing, at almost a moment's notice, the performance which brought them fame, fortune and success. *It was because they were prepared!*

It is useful here to remind you that physical exercises and/or brisk daily walking is essential to keep your body and your pelvic, gluteal and diaphragm muscles in fine trim, just as daily vocal exercises and vocalises are necessary to keep your voice in fine trim.

Exercise always in moderation, as fatigue of the body might impair your ability to control the *pelvic, gluteal and diaphragm muscles which propel the air that is converted into your voice.*

The majority of operatic artists sing only a few scales about fifteen minutes before singing an opera. There is a prevailing feeling that the highest notes (especially of a soprano) should receive extra care by not singing them more often than required.

When studying operatic roles it is advantageous to sing half-voice (mezzo-voce). You can then practice for hours if you take care to rest at frequent intervals.

Never sing your top notes needlessly while practicing, for when you do so you are wasting your voice, using something which cannot be replaced.

I am assuming that you have first learned to sing your high notes properly. After they have been firmly settled in your voice and mind, then be very sparing of their use.

Stage deportment and acting (histrionics) is a completely independent study. During this phase of your studies I recommend that you use your voice, especially your high notes, sparingly.

You will find that Richard Wagner's opera scores are clearly marked to designate his directions for the stage, but these are the exceptions. Most composers do not do so. Usually, the stage director gives you instructions which you should mark in your score accordingly.

Watching your acting in a mirror is unnecessary, because you will make the correct facial and body gestures naturally, if you have absorbed the meaning and projected yourself into the character you are portraying. Bearing in mind that you have studied thoroughly the subject of stage deportment and have learned how to fall without injury to yourself, to walk and sit down properly, and all the other ramifications involved in acting and stage deportment.

Although it is unnecessary to watch your acting or stage business in a mirror, it might be expedient to watch yourself in a mirror while singing to avoid habits such as grimacing, furrowing of brows, singing out of one side of the mouth or the raising of eyebrows, all of which are natural faults when concentrating on your work. It is *hard work* from paper to performance; *and Work, is the literal translation of Opera* from the Italian.

The Metropolitan Opera Company is constantly adding to its repertoire seldom heard, rarely performed and standard operas *sung in English.*

These translations are carefully made with especial regard to the vocal difficulties involved and the inner perception of the librettists' meanings. The day does not seem too far distant when we shall be performing all our operas in English, just as other countries, Italy, France and Germany perform their operas in their native languages. I have always and shall continue to advocate the singing of grand opera in English.

Last, but not least, I must stress that the opera singer requires and must possess a strong physical body and have enormous energy and vitality, to meet successfully the requirements of rehearsals and performances, in order to maintain and retain the beauty and quality of the voice.

CHAPTER X

THE COLORATURA SOPRANO

It is true, and proven, in this course of instruction that *voice production* is purely and simply a matter of breath, *breath control* and muscular control of the diaphragm and pelvic (supported by gluteal) muscles in *conjunction with voice placing*.

Bearing this in mind, I hereby admonish all those who possess the rare coloratura range to study this chapter carefully and diligently and to employ the instructions herein contained to the fullest, in order to use their vocal instrument to the best advantage and *preserve their voice*.

The coloratura soprano voice is rare indeed, and in a class literally by itself; and by that token, it requires and deserves particular attention in order to survive. Survive, that is, and still retain the loveliness of quality and texture as well as the range and flexibility of the voice.

In order to accomplish this end, it behooves the possessor of a coloratura voice to *build upon a firm foundation and sustain* the delicate shading required to properly execute the coloratura pyrotechnics.

104

Because the extremely high notes of coloratura sopranos have short vibrations, they *require more breath* to quicken and intensify these high notes. It is the *volume of breath* that intensifies these highest tones, when they are properly placed in the sinus cavities.

There is a prevailing misconception that the coloratura pyrotechnics are produced in the throat. Nothing is further from the truth. The variations in coloratura singing are controlled by the constant flow of breath into the resonating cavities, vibrating through the vocal apparatus enroute.

The throat of the coloratura soprano, even more than other singers, if possible, must be thoroughly and completely relaxed and free from any muscular strain, either inside or outside the throat.

Therefore, it behooves the coloratura soprano to build up the muscular control of the body, a strong and flexible diaphragm muscle and *even stronger and more flexible* pelvic and gluteal muscles. Because of their importance in singing, especially so for a coloratura soprano, *the pelvic muscles play a most important and special role.*

Pyrotechnics of the voice float out on the sustained column of air which is propelled upward by the body's muscular control, the pelvic, gluteal and diaphragm muscles, provided that the diaphragm is expanded and distended and the *lungs are filled with air.*

This muscular control is vitally important to restrain the too rapid action of the diaphragm, pelvic and gluteal muscles, so that the *breath or air flows up and out in an even controlled stream.* (See exercise for diaphragm, page 12.)

These pelvic, gluteal and diaphragm muscles *must regulate* the outgoing flow of breath which is transformed into a singing voice and upon which the coloratura proytechniques are formed into brilliant, ornamental runs, cadenzas, trills, jumps and staccatos and other embellishments that displays the singer's skill.

The coloratura soprano worthy of the name, should be capable of performing lyric and dramatic singing in opera and concert without in any way impairing or injuring coloratura singing. Therefore, it is vital that the foundation of the coloratura voice production be firmly built and be perfectly understood and applied, to preserve the rare instrument of the coloratura soprano.

The coloratura soprano, especially, must sing perfect tones which she can color and modify and spin into crescendos and decrescendos at will. These effects are produced and controlled by the manipulation of the pelvic, gluteal and diaphragm muscles to regulate the release of the breath from the filled lungs. Therefore, the pelvic, gluteal and diaphragm muscles must be so well trained and developed that they obey the will of the singer, since they control and produce these dynamic effects and proportionately intensify and modify the voice.

Especially the pelvic and gluteal muscles, *which are manipulated up and down* during cadenzas, runs and florid passages, must obey the will of the singer. (See coloratura scales with explanations.)

The coloratura soprano must first learn to sing long, sustained, even flowing tones, in the same manner as any other singer (as described thoroughly in previous chapters). I recommend the Great Major Scale (page 38) which is explained in Chapter III. The practice of this scale will equalize the entire vocal range in perfect legato singing.

Faithful practice of *interval exercises,* jumping from low to high notes and various combinations of legato and staccato is very important.

Also the *trills,* in half-tones and whole-tone intervals should be carefully practised throughout the entire range of the voice, without strain on the throat.

I remind you here, that the only place to apply pressure is on the strengthened diaphragm, pelvic and gluteal muscles.

Never press on the throat.

The throat should remain relaxed and open, a free passageway for the stream of breath from the lungs. *It is this stream of breath which is your voice, after it passes through the vocal apparatus and resonates in the bonal cavities of the head.* (See Fig. 7, page 108)

(If this chapter sounds repititious, it is meant to be so. Upon the strict obedience of all the rules laid down in this chapter depends the lasting preservation of the coloratura voice.)

The following are some vocalises and cadenzas in various scales for the coloratura soprano with directions for the muscular control of the pelvic and gluteal muscles in each scale. However, these should not be attempted until the regular scales of the female scale category in a previous chapter (see page 71) have been faithfully studied and applied.

Fill the lungs by expanding the diaphragm muscle; raise the pelvic and gluteal muscles; then sing the entire cadenza until you reach high *A*. Then relax and lower the pelvic and gluteal muscles and immediately raise and contract the pelvic and gluteal muscles while singing the balance of the cadenza.

Figure 7

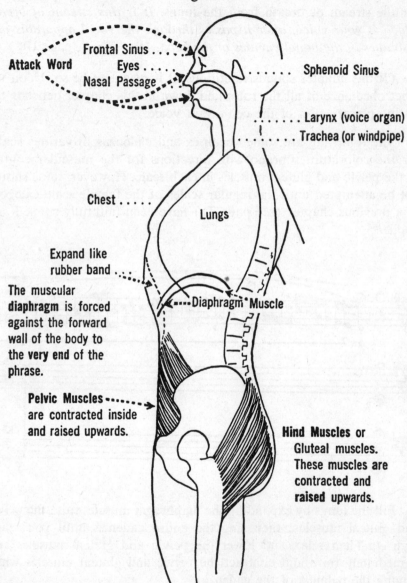

Attack Word

Frontal Sinus . . . .
Eyes . . . . .
Nasal Passage . . . .

Sphenoid Sinus

. . . . . . Larynx (voice organ)
. . . . Trachea (or windpipe)

Chest . . . . .

Lungs

Expand like
rubber band . . . :

The muscular
diaphragm is forced
against the forward
wall of the body to
the **very end** of the
phrase.

- - - Diaphragm Muscle

Pelvic Muscles - - - - -
are contracted inside
and raised upwards.

Hind Muscles or
Gluteal muscles.
These muscles are
contracted and
raised upwards.

Fill the lungs by expanding the diaphragm muscle; raise the pelvic and gluteal muscles; then sing the cadenza until you reach *B* natural. Then relax and lower the pelvic and gluteal muscles and immediately raise and contract the pelvic and gluteal muscles to finish the cadenza.

Fill the lungs by expanding the diaphragm muscle; raise and hold firmly the pelvic and gluteal muscles while singing the exercise. Sing the exercises chromatically ascending the scale until you reach high *C* or higher. Lower and relax the pelvic and gluteal muscles only on the notes at and above high *C*; quickly raise and contract these muscles during the chromatic descent of this vocalise. Apply the same theory throughout the remaining vocalises and cadenzas.

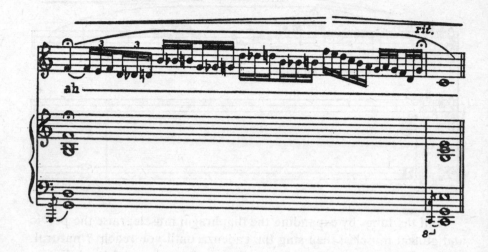

Sing the above chromatically throughout the entire vocal range, following the same pelvic and gluteal muscle manipulation.

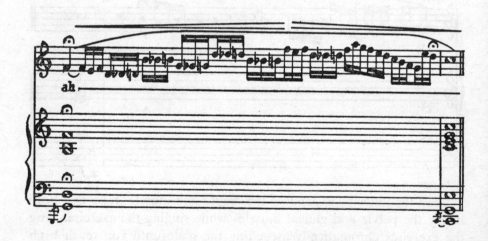

Sing the above chromatically, in one breath. Follow the pelvic and gluteal muscles directions up and down the scale.

Fill the lungs with air by expanding the diaphragm; then raise the pelvic and gluteal muscles. Sing the legato passages; then sing the staccato passages with separate diaphragm pressure on each tone.

Fill the lungs with air by expanding the diaphragm and raising the pelvic and gluteal muscles until the staccato. Then sing the staccato with separate diaphragm pressure on each tone.

Sing chromatically throughout your entire vocal range, manipulating the muscles as described previously.

See directions for other coloratura vocalises and apply to above. Practise throughout the entire range of your voice.

Sing this chromatically throughout your entire vocal range. First fill the lungs by expanding the diaphragm and contract and lift the pelvic and gluteal muscles. Only while singing high *C* and above should you relax and drop the pelvic and gluteal muscles. Then quickly raise them again when you sing the lower tones.

Sing chromatically throughout your vocal range. Fill the lungs by expanding the diaphragm; then lift the pelvic and gluteal muscles until you reach high *C* and above. Only on these very high notes should the pelvic and gluteal muscles drop down. Lift and contract them again until the end of the cadenza.

ah

See the directions for the other vocalises for coloratura and apply here. Sing chromatically through your entire vocal range without straining your voice.

Fill the lungs by expanding the diaphragm; lift the pelvic and gluteal muscles until you reach high *C*. Then relax and drop the pelvic and gluteal muscles until the end of the exercise. Be sure to sing the staccato passage by pressing out the diaphragm muscle when you sing each staccato tone.

Fill the lungs by expanding the diaphragm and lift the pelvic and gluteal muscles. Then sing the first two cadenzas. Press out the diaphragm muscles when you sing each staccato note; drop the pelvic and gluteal muscles until the end of the cadenza.

CHAPTER XI

TECHNIQUES OF
MECHANICAL VOICE PROJECTION

This is the era of high fidelity! Hi-Fi!

Just as color with its shadows and highlights are projected with perfect accuracy by the cameras upon the motion picture screen, the faithful accuracy of the reproduction of sound or air-waves, has kept pace with it, and this is called high fidelity recording.

This high fidelity recording of voices is employed presently in records, radio, television and the motion picture industry. They utilize a combination of highly sensitive microphones in conjunction with accurate magnetic tape to reproduce a lifelike, faithful recording of the voice projected.

The tapes currently used have been developed to meet the most rigid requirements of fidelity and accuracy, and in the playback they are entirely free from any and all extraneous sounds.

Even those artists who have recorded frequently in the past are startled and amazed at the results achieved by high fidelity equipment.

We can now stand off and survey our voice work and singing objectively, before we essay to record for posterity.

This high fidelity system of recording is startling because it accentuates and amplifies our slightest imperfections, as well as shows off gratefully our good qualities in equal degree.

This medium for voice projection is the most difficult imaginable. First because it shows up and amplifies our bad breathing habits, imperfections and forcing effects. A misplaced or displaced tone sounds either slightly sharp or flat in intonation; further, a tone without resonance or overtones sounds limp, and on many occasions, like an exaggerated tremolo, especially on high and sustained tones.

Air escaping around a tone (a breathy tone) produces several distorted effects such as a "hissing" sound or a "blasting" sound, depending upon the altitude and volume of the tone.

Low tones without resonance and overtones sound hollow, lacking in vitality and character, producing an excessive flatness or weakness of tone production, without any *presence*.

Good *presence* is also an important factor for recording in this medium. The technical meaning as applied to *presence* is the recording of your voice with full resonance and perfect diction, or as lifelike as possible. The effect for the listener must be as if he were standing directly in front of the singer. This is the greatest contrast to the old method of recording which sounds muted and muffled, and today's technical proficiency.

Because this medium is so sensitive and so revealing, any slight intake of breath is magnified because it breaks the melodic line of the singing and calls particular attention to a noise injected — which is what an audible breath is, a noise.

The previous chapters explained in great detail how the expansion and distention of the diaphragm muscle gives the lungs the space in which to distend also, and allows the air to rush in automatically. Therefore, there is no need to "draw in" or "suck in" the breath required for singing or speaking, especially in front of a microphone, because the air flows in by its own weight and pressure.

The position in front of the microphone is determined by the type of song or aria that you are recording, taking into account its range and its dramatic quality.

You need only step closer to the microphone when you sing the low tones (which have fewer and slower vibrations) and you must step back or turn slightly aside when you sing the highest tones, which have more vibrations, to achieve an even recording of your voice, without sacrificing the beauty and thrill of its entire range of dynamics.

A small voice, which may seem to be inadequate for concert or opera, frequently records perfectly. High fidelity recording is a boon to the singer whose voice is small and lovely in quality, provided the voice is perfectly produced, because then the vibrations are not excessive in any range of the voice.

The large dramatic voice, however, must learn to weave back and forth with the high and low tones, so that the microphone will pick up the equalized vibrations controlled by the changing position of the singer in front of the microphone.

This high fidelity era behooves us to develop our voice production and breathing apparatus to such a degree of perfection, that we can eliminate all our faults and accentuate our good points to their maximum.

We must start with our basic theory, the proper control of the pelvic, gluteal and diaphragm muscles which propel the air through the vocal apparatus, then goes on to vibrate in the bonal resonating cavities of the head to soar and float out as song from the focal point. (See Fig. 5, page 41)

This voice production will have even vibrations which will record evenly. The most gratifying result can be obtained on recording tape, because the overtones and legato controlled by the pelvic and gluteal muscles produces a beautiful melodic line of tone on the tape.

CHAPTER XII

Q . E . D .

(QUOD ERAT DEMONSTRANDUM)

Now that I have completed the expounding of the scientific theory of voice production and the perfection of technique for singing, I believe that *I have proved* the premise that *sound or voice is the resultant property of the controlled flow of air or breath.*

Secondly, *I have proved* that the *control of the flow of air or breath is solely the power of the muscular control of the pelvic, gluteal and diaphragm muscles.*

Thirdly, *I have proved that there is but one continuous register in a voice — any voice —* and that is its entire range from the top to the bottom of that voice.

Therefore, I have definitely proven the fallacy of three or seven registers which has been so detrimental and injurious to singers in the past and present, for they strive for something which does not exist.

Further, *there is only one placement for resonance,* and, that *I have proven, is in the center of the head, the sinuses, eyes and nasal cavities.*

Finally, if the scientific theories expounded in this treatise are strictly adhered to, the singer will reap the full benefits of the natural voice he or she is endowed with by nature, to its fullest extent, and will *retain the ability to preserve the voice indefinitely.*

The proof of the foregoing is that I have been singing publicly in opera, concert, oratorio, radio and on records for more than forty years and my voice still retains the youthful freshness, quality and power with which I was endowed by nature. Moreover, the critics throughout my entire career have always particularly noted the evenness of my voice range from top to bottom, my seemingly *natural legato* and my quality; in addition to praising my musicianship and interpretations.

THE END

MEMORANDUM AND NOTES

—————————————————————————

—————————————————————————

—————————————————————————

—————————————————————————

—————————————————————————

—————————————————————————

—————————————————————————

—————————————————————————

—————————————————————————

—————————————————————————

—————————————————————————

—————————————————————————

—————————————————————————

—————————————————————————

—————————————————————————

—————————————————————————

—————————————————————————

MEMORANDUM AND NOTES

MEMORANDUM AND NOTES

MEMORANDUM AND NOTES

SPECIAL DIFFICULTIES AND PROBLEMS

SPECIAL DIFFICULTIES AND PROBLEMS

_____

_____

_____

_____

_____

_____

_____

_____

_____

_____

_____

_____

_____

_____

_____

_____

_____

_____

_____

_____

_____

SPECIAL DIFFICULTIES AND PROBLEMS

_____

_____

_____

_____

_____

_____

_____

_____

_____

_____

_____

_____

_____

_____

_____

_____

_____

_____

SPECIAL DIFFICULTIES AND PROBLEMS

_____

_____

_____

_____

_____

_____

_____

_____

_____

_____

_____

_____

_____

_____

_____

_____

_____

INDEX OF SUBJECT MATTER BY CHAPTERS

132